Especially for

_____

From

_____

Date

_____

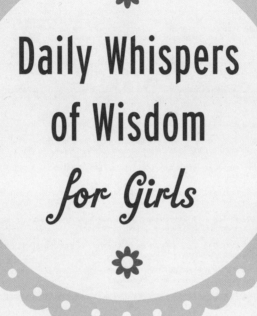

Daily Whispers
of Wisdom
for Girls

BARBOUR
PUBLISHING

Print ISBN 978-1-62029-756-8

eBook Editions:
Adobe Digital Edition (.epub) 978-1-62416-058-5
Kindle and MobiPocket Edition (.prc) 978-1-62416-057-8

Published by Barbour Publishing, Inc., P.O. Box 719, Uhrichsville, Ohio 44683, www.barbourbooks.com

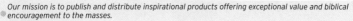

Our mission is to publish and distribute inspirational products offering exceptional value and biblical encouragement to the masses.

Member of the
Evangelical Christian
Publishers Association

Printed in China.

Introduction

*N*obody has to tell you that life is full of challenges. You're already well aware of that.

What you might need to hear, though, are some regular reminders of God's love for you. . .of the vital importance of the person you are and the one you're growing into. . .of the incredible blessings of youth in spite of the daily struggles. That's what *365 Daily Whispers of Wisdom for Girls* is all about—providing encouragement to help you face your challenges with confidence, hope, even joy.

These 365 devotional readings will turn your thoughts to the unchanging wisdom of the Bible and its heavenly Author, who longs to play a major role in your life story—the one He's written especially for you! You'll find insights into the emotions you face and practical ideas for dealing with friends, fellow students, family, and the world at large. You'll be refreshed by the real-life triumphs of other young girls and gently challenged at times to make beneficial changes to your own attitudes and actions.

Growing up has its joys and woes, laughter and tears, triumphs and trials, pleasures and pain. But with your heavenly Father by your side, you have access to all the wisdom, resources, and strength you need to accomplish everything He's called you to do—to be the best daughter of God you can be. We hope *365 Daily Whispers of Wisdom for Girls* is an encouragement along the way!

The Publishers

Happy New Year's Day

*Time is a great gift—all the more
reason to know how to use it.*

How about getting the new year off to a good start by using your time wisely? Time set aside to study for a test flies quickly with a phone call here and a text message there. But there it is, gone! So what's a girl like you to do?

Ask God to help you use time wisely before it gets away from you. Take Sundays, for example: You have at your disposal eight to ten hours. You, the daughter of the King, will definitely want to set aside some time to worship God with others in His family. Since God rested one day out of the week, why not take time to catch up on some sleep? Or perhaps make it a day to visit someone who's especially lonely.

Don't worry—there'll still be time for you to do something with your family or friends before you start back to school. When you spend each day of the new year wisely, God will keep it from getting away from you.

Whisper of Wisdom

*Teach us to number our days carefully so
that we may develop wisdom in our hearts.*

PSALM 90:12 HCSB

Welcome to the Family

*Have you ever wondered what it's
like to be adopted? Guess what? You are!*

From the pages of a storybook comes the tale of a young girl whose life is changed forever when she makes an exciting discovery. She's not just the average maiden she thought she was. She's really the daughter of a rich and powerful king.

Surprise! That maiden is you!

You have been adopted by the King of heaven. As His daughter, you now possess the keys to an entire kingdom. Imagine! Everything you need is at your fingertips! And all because you chose to be God's child. The adoption process was completed the very moment that you asked the Savior to come into your heart. He adores you! And His greatest pleasure is watching you grow and learn.

So don't think of yourself as just an average girl. Remember that you belong to a royal family. Act like the princess you have now become, and glorify the One who welcomed you with open arms into His kingdom.

Whisper of Wisdom

*Ye have received the Spirit of adoption,
whereby we cry, Abba, Father.*

ROMANS 8:15 KJV

One of a Kind

Be unique. Be original. Be yourself!

*H*ave you ever tried to be like someone else? Maybe the popular girl in school, your friend down the street, or a star on TV? Have you tried to dress, talk, or act like them? Did you think that doing so would make you happier?

Chances are, it didn't. Why? Because you are most comfortable being *yourself*!

You are a work of art fashioned by the Master Sculptor. A creation formed by the same hands that made the world and everything in it. Your creative mind. . .your serious or comical personality. . .your talents and abilities. . .all were chosen exclusively for you.

Trying to be someone you're not is like telling God that He didn't do a good job when He made you. Imagine how that makes Him feel! God wants you to shine as His creation, to develop the talents He gave you. So quit trying to be like other people. Stand out! Be different! Be *yourself*!

Whisper of Wisdom

But now, O LORD, thou art our father; we are the clay, and thou our potter; and we all are the work of thy hand.

ISAIAH 64:8 KJV

Stir Up Your Gifts!

God gave you very special gifts, talents, and abilities.
You can use those gifts to bring others into His kingdom!

Isn't it fun to think about the special talents God has given you? Maybe you can sing or play an instrument. Perhaps you enjoy acting or dancing—and love to perform on the "big stage." Maybe you prefer to scribble down your thoughts in your journal or write funny little poems to make people smile.

Remember, all of these abilities come from God, and He wants you to stir them up! Keep practicing. . .keep working at them! And while you're doing this, don't compare yourself to others. So what if someone else is a little better at something than you are? The Lord gave your friends gifts, too, and He wants those special abilities to be used. All of His children are uniquely created, and it's a blast to watch those talents grow!

The King of kings took the time to give you—His princess—gifts. Unwrap each one and use it to His glory!

Whisper of Wisdom

For this reason, I ask you to keep using the gift
God gave you. It came to you when I laid my
hands on you and prayed that God would use you.
2 Timothy 1:6 NLV

No Better Friend Than Jesus

Your friend Jesus pleads on your behalf.

The Bible teaches you not to sin and tells you what God wants you to do. But sometimes, even knowing what is right, you *may* do something wrong.

When you do, you may feel bad. That's because you know Jesus wants you to be right with God. But isn't it wonderful to know that when you make a mistake, there is Someone who will be pleading your case? It's your friend Jesus!

When you do the wrong thing, Jesus intercedes on your behalf. He pleads your case, asking the Father to forgive you.

In this world, you have no better friend than Jesus. He will always be there for you.

Whisper of Wisdom

My dear children, I am writing this to you so that you will not sin. But if anyone does sin, we have an advocate who pleads our case before the Father. He is Jesus Christ, the one who is truly righteous.

1 JOHN 2:1 NLT

Panic Attack

Everyone gets scared by something. Whether you're afraid of the dark, spiders, heights, or failure, the heavenly Father holds you in His hand.

Kara wiped her sweaty palms on her pants as she looked at the classroom clock. Three minutes till the class would line up for lunch, and Neil was standing up front, rattling on about his experiment with garden grubs. Perfect. She sighed in relief, knowing she wouldn't have to give her science fair presentation until after lunch.

It wasn't that she didn't think she did a good job on her project; it was just that speaking in front of a group of people terrified her—made her hands sweat, mouth run dry, stomach heave, and tears well up.

A few minutes later, Kara pulled her lunch box from her locker and saw a mysterious piece of paper taped over Hello Kitty's face. She looked down at the note and read: *I'm praying for you today, Kara. No matter what challenges you face, trust God to be your strength. He's with you. He loves you, and I do, too. Mom.*

Whisper of Wisdom

"Don't panic. I'm with you. There's no need to fear for I'm your God. I'll give you strength. I'll help you. I'll hold you steady, keep a firm grip on you."

Isaiah 41:10 MSG

Be Good!

Sick of everyone always telling you to be good? Feel like bending the rules just a little? Wait!

*B*efore you go too far, listen to this: The Bible tells us that if we seek good and not evil, the Lord God Himself will be with us! Don't you want to live each day knowing that God loves you and is watching over you? Then think twice before you try to bend the rules even just a little.

There will be a lot of temptations around each corner as you get older. You'll probably find that it becomes more and more difficult to "be good." Just remember to seek good, not evil, and to seek the Lord with all of your heart! God promises to be with you always (Hebrews 13:5), to provide a way of escape from temptation 1 Corinthians 10:13), and to protect you from the evil one (2 Thessalonians 3:3). With the promises of God in your heart, you'll find it a whole lot easier to "be good."

Whisper of Wisdom

Seek good, not evil, that you may live.
Then the LORD God Almighty will be
with you, just as you say he is.

AMOS 5:14 NIV

Our God Is Faithful

There are bad things all around, but God will keep you strong. Have confidence in Him!

Taylor stood next to her mother while they paid for some new jewelry. As they waited, Taylor glanced around at the items near the counter. She saw some really fun lip glosses that would be easy to sneak into her pocket. She didn't want to ask her mom to buy them. After all, she already had a box full of different flavors and colors of her favorite makeup. But she *didn't* have these. Oh, how tempted she was to add them to her collection.

Dear Jesus, she prayed, *help me to do what's right. I know stealing is wrong, but I am so tempted to take that lip gloss.*

As she finished, Taylor turned her head the other way. She knew it would be a lot easier if she turned her back on the temptation. She would have liked the lip gloss, but she liked the good feeling that filled her when she did right.

Whisper of Wisdom

The Lord is faithful, who shall stablish you, and keep you from evil.

2 Thessalonians 3:3 KJV

Practicing Your Princess Part

*How many objects are used to tell the story
"The House That Jack Built"?*

When you do a math assignment, notice the parts of your body you use. Your eyes read the problem, your mind figures out the solution, and your hand holds the pencil to write down the answer. Wow, at least three parts spring into action! Each one contributes to getting the job done. None of them can proudly say it can handle the task by itself.

God uses every part of His family, the body of Christ, to do His work. As each princess does the job God assigns her, the work will get done—if all the parts work together, that is. Your part may be to cheer others up when they're down. Another princess may befriend the new girl in your class at school. Still another may pray for U.S. troops in service overseas.

Will you pitch in as the "eye," the "mind," or the "hand" to do God's next assignment? Way to go, princess! Keep practicing your part.

Whisper of Wisdom

*All of you together are Christ's body,
and each of you is a part of it.*

1 CORINTHIANS 12:27 NLT

The Sound of a Princess's Prayer

*No use making atrocious noises when there
are so many beautiful sounds in the world.*

*D*oes the screeching sound of fingernails on a chalkboard send shivers up your spine? Oddly enough, God is set on edge by something far more serious—a prayer that tells God how much you don't need Him. Then what should a princess's prayer sound like?

One day at the temple, Jesus told a story about a man who tried to impress God with his own good deeds. Jesus explained to the crowd that such a prayer does not make a hit with God. Another man, Jesus said, simply begged God to show kindness to him, a sinner. God gladly listens to that prayer.

As God's princess, ask Him to step in and give you His goodness. Now that's a prayer that'll sound much better than fingernails on a chalkboard.

Whisper of Wisdom

*"But the tax collector stood at a distance.
He would not even look up to heaven, but beat his
breast and said, 'God, have mercy on me, a sinner.'"*

LUKE 18:13 NIV

Heaven's Bank

If you had a bank account in heaven, how much would you have saved? Jesus wants your treasures in heaven to account for more than your treasures on earth.

The news spread rapidly through the church: The Hubbards' home had burned to the ground overnight. Dan and Tina Hubbard and their two children got out safely, but little else was spared.

Members of the church quickly made sure the family's needs were provided for—doors opened to welcome the Hubbards until they figured out where they would stay long-term; clothing, household items, and food were collected and given to the family. A very scary time soon turned into a wonderful outpouring of love.

A few months later, Dan addressed the congregation during a Sunday morning service. "Almost everything my family and I owned is now nothing more than ashes in a landfill somewhere," he said. "But in some strange way, I'm thankful for that. In our darkest day, God showed that the stuff on earth is nothing. We've seen that what's truly important are the things that will last for eternity in heaven—like the love and care that you've shown us. On behalf of my wife and kids, and on behalf of God, too, thanks for showing us what it means to store treasures in heaven."

Whisper of Wisdom

"Don't store up treasures here on earth, where moths eat them and rust destroys them, and where thieves break in and steal. Store your treasures in heaven, where moths and rust cannot destroy, and thieves do not break in and steal.

MATTHEW 6:19-21 NLT

Living in Christ

The best plan for your
life is to live in Christ.

Living in Christ isn't as hard as you might think. All you have to do is believe in Jesus, love others, and obey His commands. When you do that, you will feel Him living inside of you. Wow! What a great feeling!

Some days you may end up doing things *your* way instead of *Jesus'* way, and He knows that. What Christ wants is for you to try every day to do the things He wants you to do. And He will help you. Just ask Him. Before you know it, you'll be growing in Him and finding it easier to do things His way.

You'll know it's working when you feel His Spirit deep inside of you and when you, a princess, become more like Jesus, your King, each day.

Whisper of Wisdom

Those who obey his commands live in him, and he in them.
And this is how we know that he lives in us:
We know it by the Spirit he gave us.

1 JOHN 3:24 NIV

Me, a Princess?

Don't you know? As a child of God, you are a princess in His kingdom. Yes, that's right—a princess!

On days when you're feeling down and need a boost of assurance, remember not only who you are—but whose you are. You belong to the King! He created you and made you into the unique, beautiful, and talented individual you are.

So what if you have one too many freckles? So what if you have short, unruly curls instead of long, silky locks? So what if you're not the best singer in the choir? God loves you just as you are—just as He made you. Your freckles. . .your hair. . .that off-key singing voice. . .these are things that make you different from anyone else on the planet—and all were chosen just for you by the Master Creator.

The next time you look in the mirror. . .the next time you miss that high note. . .smile, and thank God for the fine job He did making you, His princess.

Whisper of Wisdom

"I will be a Father to you, and you shall be My. . . daughters, says the Lord Almighty."
2 CORINTHIANS 6:18 NKJV

Mumbling and Grumbling

"But I don't want to! Do I have to?
Can't somebody else do it?"

Imagine this: You're taking it easy. Resting after a long day at school. Just chilling. Playing a video game. Reading a book. Talking to a friend on the phone. Then you hear those words. (You know the ones!) It's your mom's voice, and she needs you to do the dishes. Or help take care of your little brother. Or set the table.

"But I don't feel like it!" you want to say. "I did it yesterday. Ask someone else. It's *always* my turn." Maybe you even reach for the big guns, using words like "No fair!"

Here's the problem with the "no fair!" attitude—Jesus tells us not to have it. In fact, He says that we're to do everything without complaining. Sounds impossible, but we're supposed to try anyway! A princess—a true princess—doesn't mumble and grumble.

Whisper of Wisdom

Do everything without complaining or arguing,
so that you may become blameless and pure,
children of God without fault in a crooked and depraved
generation, in which you shine like stars in the universe as
you hold out the word of life—in order that I may boast on
the day of Christ that I did not run or labor for nothing.

PHILIPPIANS 2:14-16 NIV

No One Understands Me

But God does. He made you, and He
knows you better than anyone else.

On those days when everything seems to go wrong, when the day starts out great and goes downhill fast. . . When you think that no one understands you, no one knows how you feel, maybe even that no one cares—remember that the God who created you knows everything about you—even how many hairs are on your head.

He knows every feeling you have—bad and good. He knows when your day hasn't gone the way you wanted it to. He knows when your friends have let you down or when someone you counted on didn't come through for you. He knows when you think no one understands. He knows when you need to be comforted, and He is always there for you. He's just waiting for you, His princess, to bring your troubles to Him.

So the next time you feel that no one understands you, take your hurts to Him in prayer. He will understand and comfort you. He's just waiting for you to turn around. He's standing right there.

Whisper of Wisdom

"Even the very hairs of your head are all numbered."
MATTHEW 10:30 NIV

Stick Together

Your friends are priceless. You are important to them,
and they to you. Guard this treasure.

Can you imagine how sad and frightened Naomi must have felt as she prepared to leave Moab and return to Bethlehem? She dared not hope Ruth or Orpah would accompany her, and she had no one else. The life ahead would be lonely and hard.

Ruth saw that Naomi needed her. In her heart she realized that Naomi also had much to offer. It's true there were many differences between them. They probably disagreed at times, and maybe they even got on each other's nerves, but they stuck together, and both women were rewarded.

Are you ever tempted to turn your back on your friend? Maybe you're embarrassed by an outfit she's wearing, or maybe she laughed at your shoes. Has a new friend joined your tight twosome and you're feeling crowded? Perhaps your friend has developed a new interest that really doesn't excite you. Remember: There will always be differences between you. That's what makes you special. But you're a lot more alike than you realize. Don't abandon your friend. She's a gift from God, and you need each other.

Whisper of Wisdom

Two are better than one; because they
have a good reward for their labour.
ECCLESIASTES 4:9 KJV

Jesus Wants Me to Love Her?

*Some people are just so unlovable. . .
or are they? What if God loved us in the
same way that we love the "unlovable"?*

Do you know that if you have asked Jesus to have control of your life, you are considered a child of the King? Just imagine. . .He considers you a princess in His kingdom! But what about that girl in your class who doesn't dress the right way, or the one who isn't very athletic? Could *she* ever be considered a princess of the King of kings? Or does He view her as less lovable?

You probably know the answer: No one is "less lovable" to God. He created each person, and He wants to have a relationship with them. No matter how sinful they are, or how much they don't "measure up" in the world's view, God loves them and will forgive them if only they ask Him to.

Remember God's grace to you today, and pass that grace on to someone else—even someone who seems "unlovable."

Whisper of Wisdom

*If we love others, we are in the light,
and we don't cause problems for them.*
1 JOHN 2:10 CEV

The Princess Look Is In!

A princess has lots of places to shop, but wait till you hear about this exclusive design. You can't find it just anywhere.

Shucks, your favorite outfits are buried in a heap of dirty clothes, so you settle for one that's kind of blah. Time to do the laundry, right? Well, does God have the outfit for you! It's always clean and ready to put on every day. Not to worry—none of your friends will tire of it, because God makes it princess-perfect.

God wants you to step out of the flimsy outfit of despair and step into the stunning outfit of joy. With God as its designer, it'll be fashionable anytime. Joy never wears out. The more you wear it, the better it looks. Joy comes from knowing that God holds the details of your life together just like He keeps the whole world in His hands.

What a deal! Don't wait to make the switch, because you'll always look good in the Designer's outfit. It's waiting for you.

Whisper of Wisdom

The Lord has anointed me. . .to bestow on them. . .
a garment of praise instead of a spirit of despair.
Isaiah 61:1, 3 niv

God's My Boss

School might be boring. Household chores stink.
But God asks you to do work to bring glory to Him.

Sometimes it's easy to live for the future—*Life will be so much better once I'm out of this algebra class. . . . I just can't wait until middle school is over and I'm in high school. . . . When I move out of my parents' house, I'll never wash another dish again.*

The truth is that every stage of life has work and tasks that are no fun. After school comes a job; after a few childhood chores come even more chores when you live on your own. But God doesn't want you to live in misery during moments of drudgery; He wants you to work willingly, knowing that everything you do—even the boring stuff—can bring glory to Him.

Maybe the dishes stacked high in the sink or the 150 algebra problems for homework make you want to stomp your foot and scream. Don't! Take a moment to report for duty to your heavenly Boss, and get to work willingly. He's got a huge reward waiting for you at the end.

Whisper of Wisdom

Work willingly at whatever you do, as though you were working for the Lord rather than for people.

COLOSSIANS 3:23 NLT

Daddy's Girl

How beautiful you are! You look just like your Father.

*H*ave you ever compared your parents' baby pictures with yours? If so, you've probably been surprised at just how much you resemble one or both of them. Maybe you have your mom's eyes and hair color. Or maybe you got your big ears and goofy grin from Dad.

Children naturally look like their parents. And the same is true spiritually. You resemble your heavenly Father! You didn't get your freckles from God, but you did get His heart. And that means that your actions should be like His.

God is patient and kind, loving and merciful. He doesn't make fun of people or try to hurt them. He is helpful, honest, and generous. God is full of wonderful qualities—and as His daughter, you are, too! You don't have to tell others who your spiritual Father is. Your actions speak for you!

The next time someone compliments you on what a sweet young lady you are, smile and thank them. Then thank God for making you look just like Him!

Whisper of Wisdom

*Put on your new nature, and be renewed as you
learn to know your Creator and become like him.*

COLOSSIANS 3:10 NLT

Never Alone

Feeling lonely? You don't have to!
God is with you every moment of every day!

Whenever you are feeling all alone, check out Psalm 139. The Bible says that God examines our hearts and knows everything about us. He knows when we sit down and stand up, and He even knows everything we're going to say before we ever say it. Amazing! Does that make you feel closer to God and a little less lonely? If you're not quite there yet. . .keep reading. Psalm 139 continues by telling us that no matter where we go—as high up as the heavens. . .as far as the distant side of the sea. . .in the darkness or in the light—God is always with us no matter what!

We can never hide from Him, because He knows everything about us all of the time. He even knows how many hairs are on our heads (Luke 12:7)! So when you are feeling alone, remember that God is more than just the Creator of all things; He is your heavenly Father who knows you and wants to have a very personal relationship with you every day!

Whisper of Wisdom

You go before me and follow me.
You place your hand of blessing on my head.
PSALM 139:5 NLT

Prayer and Praise

Pray to the Lord and praise Him each day.

When you want to get close to a friend, you spend lots of time with her, right? The same is true of God. To get close to Him, you spend time with Him. The best way to do that is through prayer and praise.

When you pray, you can tell God all your problems. If you are having a hard time or are in trouble—in school, with your family or friends—talk it out with God and ask for His help. Before and after reading your Bible, ask God to make His words clear to you. He listens each time you call to Him, and He will help you. God always answers prayers.

God also loves to share your happiness. When good things happen to you—like getting a good grade on a test, a raise in your allowance, or that puppy in the pet store window—remember to sing songs of praise to God. Praise and thank Him for allowing goodness in your life. Praise Him for giving you a family to love, friends to care about, and happiness. If you're having a bad day and not sure what to praise, check out the psalms and read one aloud to Him. He loves to hear His Word from His daughter's lips! Afterward, you'll feel better and so will He.

The way to grow closer to God is to share your life with Him—every day.

Whisper of Wisdom

Is any one of you in trouble? He should pray.
Is anyone happy? Let him sing songs of praise.
James 5:13 niv

Playing Favorites

"Oooh, she's popular!"
"What cool clothes!"
"Here, sit by me!"

How do you pick your friends? Do you choose the cool girls, the ones in the "in" crowd?

God loves all of His princesses equally—from the most popular to the least. From the best dressed to the one in rags. From the teacher's pet to the loner. He doesn't play favorites. (He just loves you so much that it feels like you're His favorite!) He adores girls of every size, shape, and color.

God doesn't want you to play favorites. Remember that when you're tempted to hang out with someone who's popular (or cool). Maybe He wants you to spend a little time with the girl on the bus who has no friends. You know the one—she gets made fun of a lot. Get to know her, and see what God does.

Whisper of Wisdom

Suppose a man comes into your meeting wearing a gold ring and fine clothes, and a poor man in shabby clothes also comes in. If you show special attention to the man wearing fine clothes and say, "Here's a good seat for you," but say to the poor man, "You stand there" or "Sit on the floor by my feet," have you not discriminated among yourselves and become judges with evil thoughts?

JAMES 2:2-4 NIV

Princess Adrift

Some things are just too good to keep to yourself.
They're meant to be passed on to others.

You run into the mall with your mom to do a quick errand, but the pleasing aroma ends up taking you to the other side of the upper level. There you spot the just-opened kiosk selling gooey chocolate chip cookies. That aroma traveled far!

When Christ comes into your life, His sweet aroma goes farther than you think, too. People hungry for attention feel compelled to check it out. For instance, you express Jesus' love to the girl at the lunch table who pokes fun at you. Her words hurt badly, but you choose to be kind instead of getting even.

That sweet aroma will surely spread to the whole lunch table and may easily drift past the walls of the cafeteria. You never know who'll pick up on the sweet aroma of Jesus and go check it out. It may be the girl who poked fun or someone farther away who will become the next princess! Keep spreading that sweet aroma.

Whisper of Wisdom

I am grateful that God. . .helps us spread the
knowledge about Christ everywhere, and this
knowledge is like the smell of perfume.
2 Corinthians 2:14 cev

Seek and You Will Find

If you want God, He is there. He is not hiding.
He truly wants to be with you.

God loves you. He truly wants a special relationship with you, but He will never force Himself upon you. He wants you to desire His presence in your life. He has promised that if you seek Him with your whole heart, you will find Him. He won't hide in hard places; you just need to go to the right place to discover Him.

Spend some time with God today. Talk to Him in prayer. Talk to Him as you would talk to your best friend—that *is* what He wants to be. Share your joys with Him. Share your troubles. Let Him experience everything with you. Then choose a passage from the Bible, and let God talk to you.

Seek Him with your heart—you will find Him!

Whisper of Wisdom

But if from thence thou shalt seek the Lord thy God,
thou shalt find him, if thou seek him with
all thy heart and with all thy soul.

Deuteronomy 4:29 kjv

He Knows Your Needs

God meets the needs of His creation.
So don't worry—He has saved the very best for you.

Are you a worrier? Do you dwell on problems or anxieties that you cannot control but can't seem to stop thinking about?

You're not alone. Lots of people worry and fret over big and little problems, serious issues and silly things. Our heavenly Father doesn't want us to live in a state of never-ending worry. Jesus tells His followers in Matthew 6 that true believers should have faith that God knows what they need and will supply everything to meet those needs.

Worrying, Jesus said, is what unbelievers do because they don't have anyone to trust to take care of their needs. Christians have God!

So the next time nagging worry sneaks into your thoughts, take a moment to remind yourself that God already knows your needs, and He's taking care of them right now.

Whisper of Wisdom

"So don't worry. . .saying, 'What will we eat? What will we drink? What will we wear?' These things dominate the thoughts of unbelievers, but your heavenly Father already knows all your needs. Seek the Kingdom of God above all else, and live righteously, and he will give you everything you need."

Matthew 6:31–33 NLT

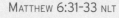

Making Less into More

Does it cramp your style to ride in an elevator?
Next time, think up five constructive things to do in that tiny space.

Maybe your family has recently moved to a smaller house, and now you share a bedroom with a younger sister. Having less space to do your thing may be a bummer, but what about putting a new spin on it? Ask God to do big things in small places.

The New Testament missionary Paul used to travel and tell people about Jesus. Think what happened to his space when his enemies threw him into jail. Before, he was free, but how could he accomplish anything now? So he asked his friends to pray that he'd have more opportunities than ever to tell others about Jesus.

Instead of focusing on the space you've lost, will you ask your princess friends to pray that you'll take on God-sized opportunities to share His love with others?

Whisper of Wisdom

Pray for us, that God will open doors for telling the
mystery of Christ, even while I'm locked up in this jail.
Colossians 4:3 msg

Your Best

Do you run the race to win?
Are you satisfied with doing just enough to get by,
or do you always give your all?

Slackers. You know who they are. Whether it's gym class, home economics, art, or math, slackers do the bare minimum—they scrape by just enough to get a passing grade. But any extra effort on their part, *no way*!

While God has given each of us special gifts and talents, that doesn't mean we should ditch everything else, not bothering to try those things outside our comfort zones and interests. Just because science isn't your thing doesn't mean you shouldn't put energy into learning it. And just because you're not into running doesn't mean you should walk the entire mile in gym class.

Every opportunity we have is from God. And He expects us to give our all in everything we do. Think about those areas in which you're tempted to slack off, and ask God for His help in keeping you motivated to give 100 percent. He won't let you down!

Whisper of Wisdom

Don't you realize that in a race everyone runs,
but only one person gets the prize? So run to win!
1 CORINTHIANS 9:24 NLT

Busy Bees

Everyone has a job to do. God has given you talents and special interests that will enable you to do what He wants you to do.

Everyone is different. We all have different interests and abilities. Some girls are musically talented; some are creative in other ways. Some do a great job with little children, and still others are better suited for different activities. No job is better or more important than another. God has designed it so that all of the jobs work together perfectly.

In a beehive, each bee needs to do his own job so that the honey can be made. The bees can't all be drones (husbands to the queen bee). They can't all be worker bees, either. And they can't all be queens. Each kind of bee is needed in order to produce the sweet, rich honey from the comb.

The body of Christ is like a honeycomb. What is it that God has set aside to be your special role? God asks you to do your best in whatever work you are given. Do it as though you are doing it for Him.

Whisper of Wisdom

Each of you has been blessed with one of God's many wonderful gifts to be used in the service of others. So use your gift well.

1 Peter 4:10 cev

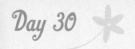

Who Shut the Door?

Sometimes God uses closed doors to keep you safe!

Ashlyn's puppy, Rosco, is a little critter who does whatever he wants. When he's not totally cuddly and adorable, he's chewing everything—trash, bugs, pretty (but poisonous) flowers, even the rubber from Ashlyn's tennis shoes. He runs in front of cars while chasing squirrels. When he's outside, a leash is the only way to keep Rosco safe.

Since Rosco loves to unroll toilet paper, burrow beneath clean bedsheets, and chew the living room carpet, many doors are closed. The only doors open to Rosco are to places prepared for his well-being—places he won't accidentally hurt himself.

Sometimes Ashlyn feels frustrated when closed doors block her from doing what she wants to do. Her mom says no to the boy-girl sleepover, the MTV program is blocked, and Dad supervises her computer time. But she knows that as with the doors she closes to protect Rosco, God uses parents to place boundaries to protect children.

So the next time you feel like whining, scratching, or howling at a closed door like Rosco, remember that some doors are *supposed* to be closed. They're part of God's plan for your protection.

Whisper of Wisdom

God is our God for ever and ever;
he will be our guide even to the end.

PSALM 48:14 NIV

Temper, Temper!

Who, me? I have a temper problem? Never!

Sometimes it's just hard to keep your temper, isn't it? Imagine this: Your little sister comes into your room and "borrows" your MP3 player—or maybe even your favorite T-shirt—without asking! Then she loses it. Loses it!

You've got a right to be mad, don't you? Surely God won't be upset if you give her a piece of your mind, tell her just what you think about what she's done.

Wrong. God doesn't want you to pitch a fit, even if you feel like you have a right to. Because you're a child of the King, He hopes you will react the way He would react. The scripture below says that He wants you to put anger and hurtful words out of your life.

So how do you do that? How do you get rid of your temper? First, you need to pray about it. Give your anger to God. Tell Him that you don't want it anymore. Then every time you start to get angry, take a deep breath and—poof!—your anger will disappear.

Whisper of Wisdom

But now also put these things out of your life:
anger, bad temper, doing or saying things to
hurt others, and using evil words when you talk.

COLOSSIANS 3:8 NCV

Role Models

Who do you look up to? Worldly women may be attractive and powerful now, but true loveliness belongs to women who love God.

Bad role models are everywhere. Just take a look at the magazines at the checkout counter or turn on the evening news. There you'll get the latest buzz about every singer/actress/model/celebrity in trouble with the law or dealing with a drug problem or generally living her private life in public.

These women may be beautiful and glamorous by the world's standards, but as daughters of God, we should want to find role models of everlasting value—the women who are beautiful because of their deep love of God and sincere faith. Who in your life has inner loveliness of love, joy, peace, patience, kindness, goodness, faithfulness, gentleness, and self-control? Maybe it's a youth group leader or a friend who is a few years older than you. Maybe it's a special aunt or your grandmother or your mom.

Take time to thank these women for their influence on your life and their commitment to showing others what it truly means to be a woman of God. Odds are, you're already a role model for someone younger than you. God wants you to show others the true beauty of Jesus in your heart.

Whisper of Wisdom

Charm is deceptive, and beauty is fleeting;
but a woman who fears the Lord is to be praised.
PROVERBS 31:30 NIV

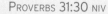

God's Far-Out Princess Plan

God likes it when someone says to you, "You know, you kind of remind me of God. Are you related to Him?"

Among other things, a princess is known by who she's related to—the king, of course! Maybe it's the color of her eyes, her smile, or a personality trait. No two ways about it; people say, "*She* belongs to the king!"

Did you know that God, the King of kings, shares His likeness with His princesses? If you are a daughter of the King, His love and kindness are bound to show up in you! The way you talk might cause others to ask about the close resemblance. God didn't throw together such a plan at the last minute. Before He created the world, way back then, He wanted you to bear His family resemblance.

God loves it, then, when someone asks you about the similarity. Your family resemblance may prompt her to become a princess, too! It's not too far out to plan for that to happen!

Whisper of Wisdom

Before the world was created,
God had Christ choose us.

EPHESIANS 1:4 CEV

Don't Do It

Don't go against what you know is right.
Don't cave to the temptation or pressure to do wrong.

Have you ever been tempted to steal something from a store. . .or even from friends? You think that the store owner will never know or that your friend has so much she won't miss what you take. Have you been tempted to tell a lie to your parents, teachers, or friends? It's easy to tell yourself that it's just a little white lie and doesn't mean anything. But a lie is still a lie. Or have you been tempted to mislead others—to trick them into doing something?

When you are tempted, when your friends are pressuring you to do what you know is wrong or to break the rules your parents have made for you, remember that you are a child of God. Even if your parents never find out, God will know. He sees everything.

Ask God for help when you're facing temptation. He loves you. And He'll help you.

Whisper of Wisdom

"Do not steal.
Do not lie.
Do not deceive one another."
LEVITICUS 19:11 NIV

Tie-Dyed Dogs

Judging by appearances is just plain wrong.

Kasie was surprised the day her next-door neighbor, a girl who always dressed in gothic clothes, exclaimed, "Sweet! A tie-dyed dog!"

Sure enough, the black fur of Kasie's dog was electrified with orange and yellow streaks. It all started when Barfy wouldn't stop chewing a hole in his back. Kasie had decided to treat Barfy's back with the hydrogen peroxide her mom had used to heal the cut on her knee.

Barfy stopped chewing, all right, but his hair turned neon!

Kasie now realized—as she fed, walked, and loved Barfy just as she had before his bad hair day—that God loves us, His children, no matter how our souls are packaged. He doesn't look at the *outside*; He looks at our *insides*. And we who love Him and want to share His love should look at others the same way.

Kasie had been afraid to speak to her new neighbor because she looked so. . .*different*. But maybe she should look at the *inside* instead.

"Want to come with me? I'm going to walk Barfy to the park."

"Sure. I like tie-dyed dogs!" Her new friend smiled. "And I've been hoping you'd ask."

Whisper of Wisdom

Don't judge by appearances.
Judge by what is right.
JOHN 7:24 CEV

Oh Me, Oh My!

Why is it that the right thing is often the hard thing?

How do you know if something is the right thing to do? Here's a little clue: The right thing is usually not easy. Example: Your friend tells a lie about you and spreads a rumor that's not true. You want to do the wrong thing—be mad at her, tell a story about her, get others as mad as you are. But God, your heavenly Father, whispers in your ear: "Do the right thing. Forgive her."

Forgive her? Are You kidding? After what she did to me?

"Yes, forgive her. That's what a daughter of the King does. She turns the other cheek."

And so you swallow hard. . .and pray. You do the one thing that's hardest to do—you forgive your friend for hurting you. And you pray that God heals your broken friendship.

Doing the right thing isn't always easy, but it's always right.

Whisper of Wisdom

I want to do what is good, but I don't. I don't want to do what is wrong, but I do it anyway. But if I do what I don't want to do, I am not really the one doing wrong; it is sin living in me that does it.

ROMANS 7:19-20 NLT

The Choice Princess

Name one thing an orchestra does
together just before a performance.
Hint: If they skip this routine, the listeners will know it.

Why did the teacher not pick *that* girl for the lead role in the play? No one could understand why she wasn't top choice. What was the teacher thinking, anyway?

That's just how the religious leaders felt when Jesus pointed to His top choice for the praise choir.

These religious men couldn't believe their eyes when they saw the honor go to little kids. After all, weren't *they*—the religious leaders—the most logical choice? The men could only see noisy brats who didn't know how to carry a tune. *Surely,* they thought, *Jesus will hush them up or send them away.*

Instead, He honors them because their hearts are in tune; and that's what God is looking for when people praise Him.

Will you be another princess to join in singing top-notch praise to God? For this choir you don't need to audition, but you want to be sure you get your heart in tune.

Whisper of Wisdom

From the lips of children and
infants you have ordained praise.
PSALM 8:2 NIV

Find Strength

When you're upset, let God be your joy.
Your delight in Him will give you the boost you need.

Cindy wasn't sure she'd ever be happy again. It had been two weeks since her grandma passed away unexpectedly, and she missed her terribly.

One afternoon after school, she found her mom sitting at the kitchen table, holding an unfamiliar Bible in her hands.

"Hey, sweetie," Cindy's mom said. "I was over at Gammy's today, and I found this Bible with your name on it. It looks like she meant to give it to you."

Cindy sat at the table and opened the soft leather cover of the well-worn Bible. Inside she found a note written in Gammy's slanted cursive writing:

My darling Cindy,
The words in this book are precious. They hold the keys to true happiness. Delight in God, and you will find delight in life—both now and in eternity with Jesus. Find your strength in these truths, and you will find true joy in your heavenly Father.
Love, Gammy

Cindy closed the Bible and hugged it close. She bowed her head and prayed silently, *Father, thank You for Gammy and her life on earth. You know how much I miss her. I'm counting on You to pull me through this sadness. You are my joy. You are my strength. Amen.*

Whisper of Wisdom

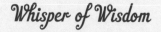

"Do not grieve, for the joy of the Lord is your strength."
NEHEMIAH 8:10 NIV

The Greatest Love

Love is a strong sentiment. It can only be truly understood when one accepts the greatest love.

There are many ways and opportunities to express your love to others. You might exchange cards with your friends on Valentine's Day. You might give your mom a stack of homemade coupons for household chores or hugs and kisses. Maybe you'll make a great big batch of chocolate chip cookies for your dad or pick a beautiful bouquet of flowers to brighten your grandma's day. These are all beautiful expressions of love, but as heartfelt as they are, they cannot come close to the perfect love God has for you.

Did you know that even when your heart was black with sin—when you were hard to love—God gave the greatest possible gift of love? He gave His perfect, holy Son, Jesus, to pay a sin debt that you would never be able to pay. What an amazing love that is! Have you accepted it?

Whisper of Wisdom

Herein is love, not that we loved God, but that he loved us, and sent his Son to be the propitiation for our sins.
1 John 4:10 kjv

Dig Deep

Patience doesn't come easily, but it's worth the effort.

*A*my could feel her temper rising as she stared at the bathroom door. "How much longer, Grandma?" she called in a razor-sharp voice. "I need to get ready for church, too!"

"Just a few more minutes, honey," a thin, wavering voice answered. "I'm moving as fast as I can."

"Arrgggh!" Amy threw the wadded-up towel she was carrying against the wall.

Dad stepped into the hall from his bedroom, buttoning his shirt.

"Amy, please try to have a little more patience."

"But, Dad, every time Grandma visits, it's wait, wait, wait! I'm tired of it!"

"You know that walker slows her down. She gets up a half hour early to finish so you can have the bathroom."

"Well, the plan's not working, Dad!" Amy bellowed, stomping her foot.

"Amy, do you think losing your temper helps anything? It only makes Grandma feel horrible. She waited on you when you were little. She had patience because she loved you and knew you were doing the best you could."

Amy thought about his words. Maybe she *should* lighten up.

"It's okay, Grandma!" she called. "I'm going to eat breakfast and then come back. Take your time."

Whisper of Wisdom

It's smart to be patient, but it's stupid to lose your temper.

PROVERBS 14:29 CEV

Love Is. . .

How do you treat your family? Your friends?
God says your love should show others His love every day.

Katie stomped into her bedroom and slammed her door—just because she could. Why was her family so dumb? Once again they made her lose her temper and say things she didn't want or mean to say.

God, I really do love them, she prayed. *It's just that sometimes I don't like them. I don't want to treat them the way I do sometimes. Please teach me how to love them the way You do.*

She opened her Bible to a chapter all about love—1 Corinthians 13. She started to write down the words that describe love.

"Love is patient and kind." *I mess that one up all the time,* Katie thought. *God, please help me learn to hold my tongue when I want to blow up at my family.*

"Love is not. . .rude. It does not demand its own way." *Ouch. The things I said to Mom and Dad tonight were definitely rude.*

"[Love] is not irritable, and it keeps no record of being wronged." *All right, God, I'm ready to make some changes. Your Word makes it easy to understand how I should love others; now I'm relying on You to help me do it. Thank You for second chances. Amen.*

Whisper of Wisdom

Love is patient and kind. Love is not jealous or boastful or proud or rude. It does not demand its own way. It is not irritable, and it keeps no record of being wronged.

1 CORINTHIANS 13:4-5 NLT

My Eternal Home

Are you a daughter of the King?
Then you have a home in heaven for all eternity!

Do you think a lot about your home? It's probably your favorite place to be—your room is exactly the way you like it, and all of your favorite things are exactly where you like them to be, right? Well, do you ever think about your *eternal* home? If we have accepted Jesus as our Savior, we get to live in heaven with Him forever after our life on this earth is over.

Jesus tells us in John 14:2 that He has gone to heaven to prepare a place for us! He is getting our room ready in heaven. Heaven is a perfect place, and it will be filled with all of your favorite things. So whenever you are having a rough day or feeling down about this life, imagine what life will be like in heaven! Remember: Jesus is getting your room ready!

Whisper of Wisdom

One thing I ask of the Lord, this is what I seek:
that I may dwell in the house of the
Lord all the days of my life.

Psalm 27:4 NIV

Keeping the Princess
Off of Dead-End Streets

What road signs are posted to give drivers a sense of direction? Hey, ask your parents!

Oops, you told your mom you knew the way to Rosa's house, but turning around in another cul-de-sac makes you wish you had listened to Rosa's directions. Now you'll be late to her birthday party.

To go the wrong way can end up costing time or even trouble. No wonder, then, that God wants His princess to look closely at His map when making life choices.

Your own map, for example, may point you in the direction of ignoring your parents' instructions, arguing with them, or disputing their word. God's map, the Bible, sends you a completely different way. In Ephesians 6:1, God directs you to the street of obedience. Obeying your parents may appear to be too far out, but trust Him. He wants to keep you off dead-end streets.

Whisper of Wisdom

I will instruct you and show you the way to go;
with My eye on you, I will give counsel.

PSALM 32:8 HCSB

Practically Perfect. . . in Every Way?

Did you know. . .that no one is perfect?

Have you ever seen the movie *Mary Poppins*? Mary describes herself as "practically perfect in every way." But is she?

Truth is, no one is perfect—except God. And it's because we're not perfect that we need Him so much! Don't let your flaws and mess-ups keep you from being all God wants you to be. After all, He doesn't expect you to be perfect.

So does that mean you shouldn't try to do the right thing? Nope! You need to keep on trying! Do the best you can. But even when you mess up (and you will), run back to Him and ask for forgiveness. You are His royal daughter, and He is your Daddy-God!

Can you imagine a young princess running into the throne room to visit with the King? That's what you do every time you spend time praying! And in that place—that throne room—He forgives all of your sins, then whispers, "I love you, daughter!"

Whisper of Wisdom

For everyone has sinned; we all fall short of God's glorious standard. Yet God, with undeserved kindness, declares that we are righteous. He did this through Christ Jesus when he freed us from the penalty for our sins.

ROMANS 3:23-24 NLT

The Greatest Love

On Valentine's Day we celebrate our love for others
and their love for us. But don't forget to tell the
One who loved you first how much you love Him!

Valentine's Day. . .a day for hearts, cards, flowers, candy, reds, and pinks. We express our love for our family, our affection for our friends, and perhaps special feelings for that "certain someone." Some messages bring smiles, and others can bring blushes and giggles in a hurry.

But take a moment to think about the One who came up with the idea of love. He made the world and everything in it–including *you*! He knew all about you before the world began. And many years later, He sent His Son to earth so that He could die for your sins. There is no love greater than that!

If you haven't already, take a few moments to thank God for His love for you. He knows everything about you, yet nothing can make Him love you any less. He will always love you–your ultimate Valentine!

Whisper of Wisdom

I want you to know all about Christ's love,
although it is too wonderful to be measured.
Then your lives will be filled with all that God is.
EPHESIANS 3:19 CEV

Listen to Your Conscience

*Your friend says yes. Your conscience says no.
Who do you listen to?*

Have you ever found yourself in a sticky situation? Maybe a friend wants you to do something wrong. Like share your test answers or lie to her parents so she won't get in trouble. What do you do? You don't want to risk making your friend mad or losing her friendship altogether. But you know in your heart that what she's asking you to do is wrong.

When you are tempted to sin—to willingly disobey the command of God—His Spirit is always faithful to caution you. That tiny voice of warning is your conscience. It stays with you no matter where you go or what you do. It's like carrying an angel in your pocket, always ready to pop out and remind you to do the right thing, regardless of the consequences.

It's always best to obey your conscience, even if it isn't easy. Your friend may be upset with you, but deep down inside, she'll respect your integrity. And she'll think twice before asking you to cheat or lie for her again.

In every situation, however sticky it may be, remember to always listen to your conscience.

Whisper of Wisdom

*"So I strive always to keep my conscience
clear before God and man."*

Acts 24:16 NIV

Mean Girls

*Some days you'll be tempted to join in when the "mean girls"
are on their worst behavior. Instead of bending under
the pressure, say a little prayer and ask God to help
you stand up for what's right. You'll be glad you did!*

You know her—the shy girl who sits in the back of the classroom. The one who gets picked last for the game in gym class. The girl who sits alone at lunchtime. The girl no one befriends for fear of being picked on, too.

Maybe there are days when you want to give her a hug and tell her that everything's going to be okay—that no one really likes those mean girls anyway. But something holds you back. You don't want to become a target for showing kindness to the class outcast.

When you're having these conflicting feelings, say a little prayer. Ask God for guidance. He's sure to point you in the right direction. And don't be surprised when you find yourself headed to the back of the classroom—with your arms open wide.

Whisper of Wisdom

*Accept one another, then, just as Christ accepted you,
in order to bring praise to God.*

Romans 15:7 niv

Invite God

God answers every invitation from His children— no matter how small the gathering.

You probably know people who are always ready for a party. They're the ones who make their way to every gathering and are always ready to hang out with anyone and everyone. Social by nature, they enjoy spending time with people and cannot wait for an invitation so they can mingle with others.

God's the same way. He yearns for the time when two or three people gather together to pray, study His Word, offer help to others, or simply spend time together in Christian friendship; and then the Holy Spirit shows up, just like that. He arrives for the smallest of meetings and the biggest of corporate worship services—they're all important to Him.

The next time you seek the presence of your heavenly Father, meet with a friend or family member or two and invite God to join you. He'll be there even before you ask.

Whisper of Wisdom

"Where two or three come together in my name, there am I with them."

MATTHEW 18:20 NIV

"I Need You, Bad!"

*Some things just can't wait.
It's kind of a now or never thing.*

Your dad or mom may give you emergency phone numbers so you can reach them anytime you're in a jam. Did you know that God has a hotline for His princess? You can reach God anytime, of course, but He really wants you to call when temptation is staring you in the face.

Instead of giving in to the temptation, tell God instantly that you need emergency help, like during a test at school. When the brainy girl in front of you leans over to pick up her pencil, you're tempted to steal a glance at her answers. Before giving in, call heaven's hotline to help you resist. God will immediately come to the aid of His princess.

It doesn't have to be a fancy prayer, just a cry for help to keep your eyes on your own test. Like your parents, God means it when He says, "Princess, call anytime."

Whisper of Wisdom

*Let us then approach the throne of grace
with confidence, so that we may receive mercy
and find grace to help us in our time of need.*

HEBREWS 4:16 NIV

Show God

God wants to know how you feel about Him,
so show Him you love Him!

You like to know that you are loved, don't you? Of course you do. Everyone does. You really need to know that God loves you. And you want to know that your parents and your whole family love you. You want to know that your friends do, too. Well, it should come as no surprise to you that God wants to know that you love Him, too.

The best way that you can show Him that you love Him, and want to be the princess He made you to be, is to obey His commands. It is not hard to do what God says He wants you to do, because He is always there to help you do it. And the more you do the things He asks you to do, the happier you will be. There is great contentment in doing God's will.

Whisper of Wisdom

This is love for God: to obey his commands.
And his commands are not burdensome.

1 John 5:3 NIV

Be Content with What You Have

God gives you what is good for you. He knows what is best.
He will always provide exactly what you need.

Your neighbor is an only child and doesn't have to share a room with her little sister. She wears designer jeans and sweaters and even has an awesome stereo. She's a nice girl, but sometimes you're so jealous of her that you can't even see her loneliness. You don't realize that while she sits in her fabulous room, listening to that great stereo, she is looking longingly at your house, thinking about how she would gladly trade her terrific wardrobe just to have a little sister.

But God knows just what is right for each of you. He knows what the future holds for you, and He commands you to be content with what He provides. Look at everything you have as a blessing from God, and use it all to glorify Him. It'll give you far more joy than wasting your time on jealousy.

Whisper of Wisdom

Thou shalt not covet thy neighbour's house. . .
nor any thing that is thy neighbour's.
Exodus 20:17 KJV

Never Give Up

What's the best thing about love?
Love rooted in Jesus lasts forever.

Love is supposed to last forever, right? The world tells us that true love will continue through anything. But in TV, movies, and real life, we see marriages split, family relationships dissolve, and friendships break up. So what good is love if it isn't lasting?

There's a big difference between what the world calls love and God's definition of love. First Corinthians 13 is known as the love chapter, and it spells out specific characteristics of love that build a foundation on Jesus. The world tells us it's perfectly natural if a husband and wife "fall out of love" or if friends have a fight and stop talking to each other. But God's Word tells us the opposite. "Love never gives up," God says. "[Love] endures through every circumstance."

Have you used the world's definition of love in your relationships with friends and family? Jesus gave us the perfect example of enduring love when He died on the cross for our sins and rose again. It isn't too late to begin again with the lasting love God wants you to show.

Whisper of Wisdom

*Love never gives up, never loses faith, is always hopeful,
and endures through every circumstance.*

1 CORINTHIANS 13:6-7 NLT

Copycat

*If you're a Christian, you are a follower of Christ Jesus.
You should imitate His character, His attitudes, and His
actions so that you'll be a good example for others to follow.*

No one likes a copycat! It is annoying to young girls when their
friends imitate them. It often creates a personal struggle to stay
unique or individual when others copy behaviors and styles, claiming
them for themselves. But you may have heard it said that imitation is
the sincerest form of flattery. This means that you should be pleased
when someone wants to be like you. It's a compliment that they like
your behavior, your style, or your words so much that they'd like to
mimic them.

Jesus wants His children to imitate Him. He has given us
perfect examples to follow by the life that He lived and through His
teachings. We show Him that we love Him when we try to be like
Him. But in order to be like Jesus, we need to spend time with Him,
studying His Word and getting to know Him better and learning what
pleases Him. Only once we truly know Him can we copy His example.

Whisper of Wisdom

*Watch what God does, and then you do it, like children
who learn proper behavior from their parents.*

EPHESIANS 5:1 MSG

Fear, Be Gone!

Need to get a really bad stain out?
One that won't wash away on its own? Out, spot! Out!

Have you ever seen those commercials for spot-remover—the handy-dandy stuff that's guaranteed to get out even the toughest stains? It seems to work like magic (at least on TV). Wow!

Do you wish you had a "fear-remover"—something you could use to wash away all of your worries and fears in a hurry? Well, guess what—you do!

When you put your trust in God, you have nothing to be afraid of. Scared of the dark? Fear, be gone! Scared of school? Fear, be gone! Scared of failing or being embarrassed around others? Fear, be gone—in Jesus' name!

God never intended for His kids to live in fear. In fact, faith is the opposite of fear. So the next time you start to get afraid, remember: God is your light and your salvation. Just look at that thing you're scared of and speak these words: "Fear, be gone—in Jesus' name!"

Whisper of Wisdom

The Lord is my light and my salvation—
whom shall I fear? The Lord is the stronghold
of my life—of whom shall I be afraid?

PSALM 27:1 NIV

A Delicate Step

It's not an ordinary walk that's challenging; rather, it's the agile step that calls for patience and practice on the part of a princess.

Whether you watch or participate in ballet, it doesn't take long to notice the ballerina's pointed toes or graceful steps. These delicate moves come with time and practice, though at first they look to be impossible. It's the same when God invites you to practice the delicate maneuvers of sharing your faith in Christ with your family or friends. *How do I do it?*

It takes practice to step into someone else's space and talk about Jesus. But when you try, God will help you stand up for Him in places you can hardly believe. It may feel awkward at first, but God sees that you want to stick with it. Not to worry—He's with you every step of the way.

God invites you, princess, to come out for practice. Are you willing to move about in unsure places to share Jesus with others gracefully?

Whisper of Wisdom

He makes my feet like the feet of a deer and sets me securely on the heights.
PSALM 18:33 HCSB

Make Me a Servant

Jesus loved His enemies—even those who put Him on the cross. He asks the same of you. Will you listen?

Allison dreaded walking in the hallways between biology and lunch because she knew she couldn't avoid Missy. Every day Missy asked—well, demanded—that Allison give her half of her lunch money. What would happen if Allison refused? Missy was big and mean, so Allison decided she didn't want to find out.

Soon Allison realized that Missy was using the dollar to buy whatever she could in the cafeteria. It usually ended up being fries or an ice cream sandwich—never enough food to satisfy Missy's appetite.

Allison decided to start packing her lunch. The first day she included an extra sandwich, yogurt, juice box, and carrots. Like clockwork, Missy stopped Allison on her way to lunch and demanded money.

"Sorry, Missy, but I packed lunch today, so I don't have any money." Allison winced, thinking Missy might hit her. "But if you want, I'd be happy to share what's in my lunch."

Missy narrowed her eyes and bit her lower lip, as if considering whether to take Allison's offer or hit her to teach her a lesson. "Yeah, okay," she finally said. "Whaddya got?"

Whisper of Wisdom

"Love your enemies. Let them bring out the best in you, not the worst."

Luke 6:27 MSG

W for Worthy!

Can you hear it? The rocks along the edge of the road. . .
They're singing the praises of God!

Did you know that we were created to worship God? It's true! If we don't praise Him, the rocks will begin to shout out praises to the King of kings. (Can you imagine the rocks bursting out in joyful song? Wouldn't that be something to hear!) We're going to be praising the Lord for all eternity, so we'd better get started now.

God is worthy to be praised! He's amazing and awesome. He created the whole world—just by speaking it into existence. He sent His Son to die on the cross—proving His love for us, once and for all. Yes, God truly loves us, and that alone makes Him worthy!

A daughter of the King can't say enough good things about her Father. Why, she brags on Him all day long! She sings His praises to everyone who will listen. So let a song of praise fill your heart today, princess. If you don't, the rocks will surely begin to shout!

Whisper of Wisdom

I call to the LORD, who is worthy of praise,
and I am saved from my enemies.

PSALM 18:3 NIV

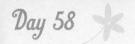

Lost!

God is true to His promises.

Mandie was terrified. She'd used her white cane to enter the building as her teacher for the blind had taught her, but now she was hopelessly lost and alone.

"Hello," she called in a shaky voice. "Anybody here?"

Nothing but a loud grinding sound greeted her. It sounded like—*gulp*—a chain saw. Had she misunderstood the pastor's announcement that the middle school group would meet in the new youth building? Where was everybody?

Mandie had insisted that Mom drop her off so she could enter by herself, just like everyone else. She wanted more than anything to feel like a regular kid. But now she was in trouble!

"God," Mandie prayed aloud, her voice swallowed by the horrible noise, "You said we can trust You when we're afraid. That would be now, Lord! Please send help!"

Suddenly the noise quieted and Mandie heard a door slam, followed by running footsteps. Was it a crazed madman with his chain saw?

"Mandie, there you are!" The voice of Mandie's friend Kristin never sounded so sweet. "I've been looking for you—everyone's out back playing volleyball while the workmen check the emergency generator." She took Mandie's hand. "Come this way!"

"Thanks, Kristin!" Mandie said with immense relief. "And thanks, Lord!"

Whisper of Wisdom

What time I am afraid, I will trust in thee.

PSALM 56:3 KJV

Brighten Up, Princess!

If God is in your thoughts, will He show up on your face?
He has a beautiful expression for you!

If you feel anxious today, take a minute to adjust the zoom lens on the pictures popping into your mind. Instead of zooming in on the details of your troubles, ask God to move front and center. Your expressions of worry and tension will slip into the background as God brightens your face to shine like the sun.

Because you are His princess, God wants to help you work out the things that trouble you as soon as you ask. For example, if your soccer team, with a 3-0 record, loses the next game, pictures of anger, envy, or disgust may flash into your mind. You may be tempted to press on the zoom button until all you see are the things that upset you. Why not zoom out on this stuff and bring God up close to help you through the disappointment?

Your new focus won't change the score, but it will transform your "out" look. God's always ready to brighten up His princess!

Whisper of Wisdom

Those who look to him for help will be radiant with joy;
no shadow. . .will darken their faces.

PSALM 34:5 NLT

High-Heeled Sneakers

Don't be so hasty to trade your sneakers and play clothes for high-heeled shoes and lipstick. Everything has its moment and purpose. You are right where God wants you to be—enjoy it!

*T*ime goes so fast! You probably hear that from grown-ups all the time. It's true, though. In the blink of an eye, you will be looking back with longing for the days of sneakers and skinned knees while you are rushing out the door to work. You hang in a delicate balance right now. You're too young to be old, but you feel too old to be young. So what do you do?

Take things slowly. Embrace and enjoy exactly where you are, in the very moment you are, for it will pass before you know it. There is no need to rush the high heels, the makeup, the boyfriends—all of those things will come in their due time. Patience will produce God's perfect result in your life. Impatience will rob you of lasting childhood memories, upon which you can build a lifetime of joy and faith.

Whisper of Wisdom

Let patience have its perfect work, that you may be perfect and complete, lacking nothing.

JAMES 1:4 NKJV

Playing Grown-Up

*High-heeled shoes. . .fancy dresses. . .
a little girl acting all grown up. . .*

Playing "grown-up" is a lot of fun when you're little, isn't it? Wearing your mom's shoes. . .dancing around the house in one of her pretty dresses. It's a blast to act like an adult!

Sometimes we get so excited about what it's going to be like when we're older that we forget God created children for a reason. He likes it that you're not grown-up yet, and He's in no hurry to get you there!

Don't ever look down on yourself because you're young. This breaks God's heart. Don't ever say, "But I'm just a kid! What can I do for God?" The truth is, you can do plenty! And He wants you—no, He *needs* you—to understand that you don't have to wait till you're grown up to tell others about Him. So start now. Right where you are. Kick off those high-heeled shoes, grab your tennies. . .and get running!

Whisper of Wisdom

*But the LORD said to me, "Do not say, 'I am
only a child.' You must go to everyone I send
you to and say whatever I command you."*

JEREMIAH 1:7 NIV

Peace Comes from Doing God's Will

The peace that passes all understanding can be yours.
Love God's Word and learn it.

Do you ever feel uncomfortable because some of your friends want you to do something you don't think you should? Or have you felt confused because you aren't sure what it is you should be doing? Do you feel worried that you might do something wrong just to please others? Do you need direction from a master navigator?

To figure out which way to go on the road of life, check out God's Word. It has all the direction you need. The more you read and study your Bible, the better you will know what you should and shouldn't do. And His Word will also give you the strength to tell yourself or your friends no when you need to.

Want peace of mind? Just pick up your Bible and then talk to Jesus—the Prince of peace. They'll give you good directions to follow, the strength to obey, and the peace that comes from choosing the right path.

Whisper of Wisdom

Great peace have those who love Your law,
and nothing causes them to stumble.
PSALM 119:165 NKJV

Got Hope?

Do you have Jesus in your heart?
He is our only hope for the future.

When you ask Jesus to come into your heart and take away all of your sins, the Holy Spirit comes and makes His home inside of you. God pours out His love into our hearts by giving us the Holy Spirit to live inside our hearts. The Holy Spirit gives us hope for the future and helps us to know right from wrong.

Do you have the hope of knowing you will spend eternity with Jesus? If not, take the time right now to ask Him to come into your heart. You can pray a prayer something like this: "Dear Jesus, thank You for dying on the cross for my sins. Please forgive me for all the bad things I've done, and send the Holy Spirit to come and live in my heart so that I can be with You someday. Amen."

If you have prayed that prayer for the very first time, go tell your parents or someone you trust from church. Ask them to help you get to know Jesus better!

Whisper of Wisdom

Hope does not disappoint us,
because God has poured out his love into our
hearts by the Holy Spirit, whom he has given us.
ROMANS 5:5 NIV

Stand on the Truth

Do you know what the Bible says? Read it.
Ask God to help you understand it.

*D*o you make time every day for reading the Bible? You know it's the only way to find out what God expects from you. Not only that, but you will be full of joy just from spending time with Jesus. A lot of people might tell you that it's hard to understand God's Word, but it really isn't—not if you really want to. All you need to do is ask God to show you what He means. He'll be glad to help you figure it out. And you know something else? The more you read, the more you'll understand.

It's very important for you to do this, because there are lots of people who are teaching things that aren't really in the Bible. It's Satan's way of distracting us from the truth, but if you know what's in the Bible, you'll be able to spot the phony stuff when it shows up. So be prepared. Read the Bible and spend time with the Author.

Whisper of Wisdom

Be not carried about with diverse and strange doctrines.
For it is a good thing that the heart be established with grace.

HEBREWS 13:9 KJV

Head Scratchers

It's impossible to understand everything about God. For now He asks us to trust Him until He answers all our questions in heaven.

Have you ever tried to understand—really, truly understand—God? Little kids ask their parents, "Who is God's mommy?" and "Could there ever be a rock so big that even God couldn't lift it?" The answers to these questions go against everything we know as humans: God doesn't have a mommy; He has always been there. God can lift the biggest rock that there ever could be.

God's love for us sinful humans is just as confusing. The Master Creator loves His creation so much that even when Adam and Eve sinned, God said, "Yes, you messed up. But I love you so much that I have a plan for us to be together." That plan is Jesus.

Someday in heaven the fog of confusion will lift. We'll understand God's will and His plan for all of creation. We'll know why He answered our prayers the way He did. And we'll fully understand how big His love is for us.

Whisper of Wisdom

We don't yet see things clearly. We're squinting in a fog, peering through a mist. But it won't be long before the weather clears and the sun shines bright! We'll see it all then, see it all as clearly as God sees us, knowing him directly just as he knows us!

1 Corinthians 13:12 msg

Going against the Flow

Everyone else is doing it. So why shouldn't you?

*E*verybody lies. Everybody cheats. Everybody disobeys their parents. . .or do they? And even if that's true, is it okay for *you* to do those things?

Many people like to say that "everybody does it" to excuse their own bad behavior. But the truth is that when you are a child of God, you are expected to do *His* will. That means telling the truth even if no one else does. It means refusing to cheat and always obeying your parents. It means not stooping to the level of "everybody."

God's children are different because they *act* differently than the rest of the world. They go against the flow. They stand up for what's right. They are honest and obedient, even if being so makes them unpopular.

God treasures His children. He blesses them for their obedience. He takes care of their needs and makes sure they are happy. And best of all, He promises a wonderful reward in heaven someday.

Don't be like "everybody." Be bold. Be different. Be a child of God.

Whisper of Wisdom

"Now if you will obey me and keep my covenant,
you will be my own special treasure."

Exodus 19:5 NLT

The Princess Cup

When you invite friends to a princess tea party, you surely don't want to run out of tea. How about a bottomless teapot?

As you hurry to get ready for school, you pour some breakfast cereal into your bowl and realize somebody left you with a few drops of milk. Then you get to class forgetting you used up your notebook paper. Nearly everything eventually runs out. So does anything simply keep on giving? You'll love the answer, princess. God's love never runs dry!

God's love is plentiful in the morning, there for you at bedtime, and available every minute in between. Don't worry about the next day, either, because it'll never get down to the last few drops. There's plenty to go around. God loves you with a bottomless love that keeps on giving.

As you get into the day and things run out, pause and thank God for His awesome supply of love. Enjoy! You'll never use it up!

Whisper of Wisdom

"I have loved you with an everlasting love."
JEREMIAH 31:3 NIV

"But Her Mom Lets Her!"

God has expectations for your parents. But He also has expectations for you. Will you do your part?

Have you ever spoken those words to your parents when trying to get their permission to do something you *really* want to do? Maybe it's watching a certain movie, or buying that outfit you've been wanting, or going to a friend's party—something you just *have* to do.

And then their answer drops like a hammer: "No." Do they forget what it's like to be your age? Or do they just not want you to have any fun?

Actually, it's neither. Your parents want what is best for you. They have grown in wisdom over the years, and God expects them to be wise in how they raise their kids. But He also wants certain behavior from their kids, too: He wants you to "honor your father and mother." That isn't obedience only—it's obedience with respect. God doesn't say it will be easy, but it *is* what He commands.

Whisper of Wisdom

*"For God commanded, saying,
'Honor your father and your mother.'"*
MATTHEW 15:4 NKJV

Follow the Leader

When God is our leader, we can't fall.

*T*hick fog covered the high mountain trail like a white blanket. Faith's church youth director, Joshua, reminded the fourteen fifth-graders hiking behind him to be careful where they stepped.

"It would be easy to become careless and stray off the path in conditions like this. You wouldn't know you were at the edge of a cliff until you tumbled off the side."

Faith's breath caught in her throat. She hadn't planned on dying today!

"Form a single line and join hands," Joshua instructed. "I know exactly where we're headed, and if you follow directly in my footsteps, you'll all make it to the top."

Faith felt her hands gripped by Lexie on her left and Eric on her right. At that moment, Faith tripped over a rock, but Eric and Lexie kept her from falling.

"You know, this is like living a Christian life, isn't it?" Joshua's voice echoed off the canyon walls. "God knows exactly where we're headed. If we make sure our feet follow in His path and we're supported by other believers, we may stumble, but we won't fall."

Thank You, Lord, Faith prayed silently, *for keeping me safe on Your path.*

Whisper of Wisdom

Know where you are headed, and you will stay on solid ground.

PROVERBS 4:26 CEV

A Spoonful of Sugar

A little kindness goes a long, long way.

Has your best friend ever suddenly decided she didn't want to be your friend anymore? Happens all the time, doesn't it? People who start out as friends sometimes end up as enemies. In fact, things can get pretty ugly.

It breaks God's heart when people don't get along. He wants His kids to love one another. But how is that possible, especially if people are mean to you? What can you do to make things better?

The next time someone mistreats you, instead of getting mad, try a little kindness. The Bible says we should not return evil for evil. It doesn't help things to treat the other person badly, after all. In fact, it just makes things worse!

This might sound crazy, but next time, do something nice for the person who is treating you badly. Write her a nice card, or give her a small gift (maybe something that means a lot to you). Just watch and see if a little kindness doesn't go a long, long way in making things better!

Whisper of Wisdom

If your enemy is hungry, give him food to eat;
if he is thirsty, give him water to drink.

Proverbs 25:21 NIV

Accepting Change

Change is tough to face. It's important to remember that even in the face of change, God's will is at work.

Are you facing some kind of change in your family? Maybe you've had to move to another city, change schools, and make new friends. Maybe the structure of your family has been changed by death or divorce. No matter what changes you are facing, you should remember that if you know Jesus, your life belongs to Him. And even in the midst of change, God's will prevails. Sometimes He allows change so that you will become stronger. And sometimes it's so that you will be able to help others who may go through something similar.

God is never careless with His children. Things don't happen by accident or because He forgot to pay attention. He is fully aware of what's happening in your life. And more important, nothing can come into your life that doesn't pass by Him first. So don't struggle against His plan for you. Realize that you're God's special treasure. He knows what's best for you, and He'll take care of you no matter what changes come your way.

Whisper of Wisdom

This is the day the LORD has made.
We will rejoice and be glad in it.
PSALM 118:24 NLT

Honor Your Parents

Respect for your parents is required by God. He put you together for a purpose. Obey Him, and He will bless you.

Maybe your parents are totally great. Yours is the house where all the kids want to spend their time. On the other hand, maybe you feel like your parents are trying to rule your life. Or it could be that your mom and dad fall somewhere in the middle.

The truth is that no parent is completely perfect. Parents are human just like you are. For the most part, they are trying to help you become a mature young woman. Even though you might not like everything they say or do, you must remember that God has a reason for putting you together. He expects you to honor your parents—to respect and obey them.

When things go well, thank God. If you are struggling, turn your situation over to God. You might be surprised to discover that it's you who needs to change.

Above all, honor your parents, and enjoy God's blessing that follows.

Whisper of Wisdom

Honour thy father and thy mother, as the Lord
thy God hath commanded thee; that thy days may
be prolonged, and that it may go well with thee,
in the land which the Lord thy God giveth thee.

DEUTERONOMY 5:16 KJV

Heartfelt Praise

God's ears don't hurt if your pitch is off.
He desires your deep, heartfelt praise, however you give it.

Joanna always found an excuse to skip the first fifteen minutes of Sunday night youth group. That's when everyone sang a few praise songs to an acoustic guitar.

It's not that I don't want to worship God, she reasoned, *but I can't sing. I don't want to make everyone else listen to my voice. I sound like a bullfrog.*

Soon the youth group formed a praise band to lead songs every week. Joanna volunteered to be the drummer. *This is one way I can keep people from hearing me sing,* she thought.

Joanna loved the songs the band played, but she found herself disappointed that she couldn't praise God the way everyone else did.

"Singing isn't the only way to praise," her youth sponsor said. "God loves hearing you whale on the drums when you're doing it to glorify Him. Joanna, it's not about music; it's about your heart."

What about you? Making music to the Lord could mean singing or playing an instrument or clapping or dancing or painting or writing—the options are endless. God's desire for you is to find the music of your heart and play to His glory!

Whisper of Wisdom

Be filled with the Spirit. . . .
Sing and make music in your heart to the Lord.
Ephesians 5:17-19 niv

Good Deeds

*The good things that you do are never "in vain"
when they are done for Him. When God gives
you a task, carry it out with all your strength.*

A young girl once decided to help an elderly neighbor by clearing her sidewalk after a snowstorm. A little later in the day, she learned that her neighbor was out of town for the week. The girl was very disappointed, because by the time her neighbor returned from her trip, the snow likely would have melted and she would never know what the young girl did to help her.

Sometimes we do things that we think will receive the praise and thanks of others. My, how surprising and disappointing it is when those good deeds go seemingly unnoticed!

But in truth, the good things we do for other people are actually done as though they are for the Lord. He sees our deeds, and the only rewards we should want are from Him.

We help others because we know God will use our efforts to bless them, maybe now or maybe years from now. He doesn't waste any work that's done for Him, and He always rewards a giving heart.

Whisper of Wisdom

*"Be especially careful when you are trying to be good
so that you don't make a performance out of it."*

MATTHEW 6:1 MSG

The Princess's Claim to Fame

There's nothing like knowing you belong, that you matter to someone enough for them to make room for you.

After landing at an airport, you and your family make your way to the baggage claim. As your suitcase topples its way onto the carousel, imagine it wondering if it will be claimed by its owner. After all, lots of luggage is piling up, but it hopes you find it because it isn't fun to go in circles. What a relief it is when you take hold of it because it belongs to you.

In a way, that's what God does for you. The Bible says He wants to claim you to be with Him instead of letting you go around in circles. God identifies you as His. What an honor for God to claim you!

Unlike your imaginary thinking suitcase, you can trust God to come back for you to be with Him. God reaches out to you every day and invites you to go with Him instead of wandering hopelessly. You'll always know where you belong—with God.

Whisper of Wisdom

From the beginning God chose you to be saved.
2 Thessalonians 2:13 niv

A Thankful Heart

When things don't quite go your way, instead of feeling sorry for yourself, think of everything in your life that's good—there are a lot of wonderful things in this life of yours! Then say a great big thanks to God.

*B*ad days? We all have them. And you've been there with. . .the haircut that didn't turn out like the picture, the reprimand from your teacher for talking in class, the less-than-perfect grade on your spelling test, and the bruised knees from your embarrassing trip over your chair in Sunday school.

We can't always control things that go wrong, but we can control our reaction to those things. So the next time you have a bad day, think about the wonderful things in your life—like your wonderful family, your cuddly pet, your best friend, your bedroom that's decorated just the way you like it—and you'll find yourself bouncing back fast from your sour mood.

And last but not least, thank God for all the good stuff in your life. He'll be happy to hear from you!

Whisper of Wisdom

Always give thanks for all things to God the Father in the name of our Lord Jesus Christ.

EPHESIANS 5:20 NLV

An Undivided Heart

It's not possible to fully serve two different masters. The Lord requires an undivided heart of service and worship to Him.

Is your heart divided between two masters? Does God receive a small piece of your devotion while you keep the rest for yourself? Having a divided heart—one that is not fully and solely in the Master's hand—is a very risky way to live. God doesn't require your complete devotion for any other reason than as a way to provide for you. He knows that He watches out for you like no one else will. And He knows that He can be trusted with your heart like no one else can. By asking for your complete devotion, He is offering you His divine protection.

But God doesn't want your devotion because you *have* to give it. He wants you to *want* to be with Him and to want the things He offers you. It may seem like you have to give up a lot to follow Jesus. But the eternal rewards are much better than anything you might lose in this world.

Whisper of Wisdom

Everything you do or say should be done to obey Jesus your Lord. And in all you do, give thanks to God the Father through Jesus.

COLOSSIANS 3:17 NCV

Star Light, Star Bright

Shining, glimmering, twinkling.
Brightening the darkness. That's what you do!

Have you ever looked at the sky at night? If you live in the city, chances are that you can't see very many stars. But if you get away from the streetlights of town and gaze at the same sky, you'll be amazed. Millions of stars, like scattered diamonds, shine in the heavens, brightening the darkness.

As God's child, you are like one of those twinkling stars. His light shines within you, visible to all who see. And each time you tell the truth. . .each time you show kindness to others. . .each time you obey God's Word, your light shines brighter. And just like the stars in the sky, you are most visible when surrounded by darkness. When others do the wrong thing but you stand up for what's right, your tiny glow becomes a beacon.

So don't be afraid to do what's right, even if no one else does. Remember that you are a glittering diamond in the night sky. Keep shining. Keep sparkling.

You glow, girl!

Whisper of Wisdom

Become blameless and pure, children of God
without fault in a crooked and depraved generation,
in which you shine like stars in the universe.

PHILIPPIANS 2:15 NIV

Practice Makes Perfect

Things to practice:
the piano, the violin. . .truth?

A daughter of the King always tells the truth, even when it's hard. Why? Because it's the right thing to do. We can't go around telling people we're Christians if we're not going to act like it. Our words and actions have to match up.

Imagine meeting a new girl at school. She tells you she's a Christian, and you're excited to have a new friend. You sit next to each other in class and even invite her to your house for a sleepover. Then you see her doing something really bad—maybe lying to the teacher or stealing something. You're confused by her actions. They don't match up with her words. She said she was a Christian, but she's not acting like one.

It's time to speak the truth in love. Remind your friend of what the Bible says. We have to let the light of truth shine bright! So start practicing!

Whisper of Wisdom

This is the message we heard from Jesus and now declare to you: God is light, and there is no darkness in him at all. So we are lying if we say we have fellowship with God but go on living in spiritual darkness; we are not practicing the truth.

1 JOHN 1:5-6 NLT

Little Biddy Buddy

*If God takes care of the birds
we know He watches over us, too.*

Mr. Peepers started out as a tiny, fluffy Easter chick. He went with Kristin everywhere, sitting beside her on the couch to watch TV, cuddling on her pillow at night, even following her into the shower. He loved to roost on her basketball like it was an enormous orange egg!

Mr. Peepers grew into a fine young rooster, and one morning, he began crowing. His *Err-er-errr* at sunrise woke all the neighbors, and Kristin knew it was time for Mr. Peepers to go to a farm. But when the day came, she didn't want to leave Mr. Peepers and he didn't want to leave her. He chased Kristin's car down the farmer's dirt driveway while she tearfully waved good-bye from the back window.

Kristin prayed that God would take care of Mr. Peepers, and He did. The farmer said Mr. Peepers made friends with all the cute chicks and became the king of the chicken coop.

Kristin learned that the Bible says God knows when every sparrow falls to the ground. She knew that if God cared that much for sparrows and Mr. Peepers, He would take care of her, too!

Whisper of Wisdom

*"Don't be afraid, you are worth
more than many sparrows."*

Matthew 10:31 NIV

He Hears Me

God eagerly desires to answer your requests.
Don't wait any longer to talk with Him in prayer.

Did you know that God *enjoys* hearing us ask Him for things that please Him? When we make requests that are within His will, He hears us and will give us what we ask for.

God isn't a heavenly Santa Claus, though. Our requests for new clothes, jewelry, and cell phones aren't the prayers He's ready to answer. Instead, the prayers He's eagerly waiting to hear are the ones that you pray on behalf of someone hurting or in need. Selfless prayers are melodies He longs to hear.

Or maybe you're looking for guidance about a decision you need to make—ask God. Ask Him for the wisdom you need to live out His will every day. Ask Him to supply the things you need, having faith that He's already working out everything before you even know you have a need.

More than anything else, God wants to hear from you. Talk to Him today, and then take time to listen for His voice.

Whisper of Wisdom

We are confident that he hears us whenever we
ask for anything that pleases him. And since we
know he hears us when we make our requests,
we also know that he will give us what we ask for.
1 JOHN 5:14-15 NLT

Should I. . .or Not?

*Jesus faced temptation just like we do.
In our response to it, we should choose to follow His example.*

Is temptation a sin? No, being tempted isn't a sin; we only sin when we give in to temptation and do something that God doesn't want us to do. Jesus Himself was tempted. But each time He faced temptation, He quoted scripture. He did not give in to Satan's demands; He referred to His Father's power.

The Bible says in James 1:13 that when we are tempted, we shouldn't say that God is tempting us, because He cannot be tempted, and He doesn't tempt anyone. Temptation is only from the devil, who wants to lead us away from Christ.

The next time you face temptation, quote scripture, such as Matthew 4:10: "Worship the Lord your God, and serve him only" (NIV). Then run from the temptation as fast as you can!

If you give in to temptation, ask Jesus to forgive you and to give you the strength not to repeat your mistake.

Whisper of Wisdom

*You are tempted in the same way that everyone
else is tempted. But God can be trusted not to
let you be tempted too much, and he will show
you how to escape from your temptations.*

1 CORINTHIANS 10:13 CEV

The Princess Dig

What makes you say, "Hey, that tastes so good;
I'm going back for more"?

Once you take a bite of your favorite ice cream, no one has to talk you into the next bite. You've already found out that it's good. Imagine, then, how happy God is when you come back again and again for "more" of Him.

It's awesome to come to God through His Son, Jesus Christ, but there's so much more to discover. That's only the "first bite" of many good things to come. By digging into the Word of God regularly, you'll grow in your faith and keep learning how to trust God more with what's going on in your life. What happens when you learn about the goodness of God? You'll want to come back for more.

Hungering for more because you love God will keep your faith and trust in Him going strong. Are you ready to dig in for more?

Whisper of Wisdom

But you, dear friends, build yourselves
up in your most holy faith.

JUDE 20 NIV

God-Pleasers!

Are you a people-pleaser? Always trying to make everyone happy? Guess what? That's not your job!

God wants us to please Him first! It's not our job to make everyone happy.

As you get older, there will be lots of times when God's Word goes against what all of your friends are doing. Sometimes grown-ups and other people you trust might be going against God's Word, too! How will you know? Ask God to help you know right from wrong and keep His Word in your heart. If you study God's Word every day, you will know when other people are going against what the Bible says.

If all of your friends decide to cheat on a test at school, they won't be very happy if you tell them it's wrong and you aren't going to do it. But that's okay! It's not your job to make everyone happy. It's much more important to make God happy than all of your friends. All you have to do is trust God and do what's right. That's all that matters in the end!

Whisper of Wisdom

Obviously, I'm not trying to win the approval of people, but of God. If pleasing people were my goal, I would not be Christ's servant.

GALATIANS 1:10 NLT

Praiseworthy

We must remember to give God our praise. He is our Creator and our Father in heaven. Without Him, we wouldn't be here.

Sometimes with all the things going on in our world, we can forget how awesome our God is. We can get distracted with TV shows, video games, clothes, and other worldly stuff. But God doesn't want us to pay so much attention to those things that they become idols to us. He does not want them to become more important than He is.

God created the heavens and the earth. He made the world we live in. No one else did. He's the ruler of the universe. And you are a princess of His kingdom. How cool is that? Yay, God! He is the great "I Am."

How can you show Him He's more important to you than anything else? How about getting away from the TV for a while and spending some time praising His name and being thankful that God loves you.

Give praise to your King. He loves hearing you cheer Him on!

Whisper of Wisdom

*Great is the LORD and most worthy of praise;
he is to be feared above all gods. For all the gods of
the nations are idols, but the LORD made the heavens.*
1 CHRONICLES 16:25-26 NIV

Words That Judge

The things you say reflect the condition of your heart.
Be careful with your speech so that you
always bring honor to Jesus.

Do you avoid using swear words? How about words like *gosh*, *golly*, and *gee*? These words are shortcuts for names of God or Jesus. Those are things that you may say or think without being aware of their true meaning, but how about other words? Swear words, curses, lies, sarcasm, disrespectful speech, mocking, and insults are all examples of words that may come out of your mouth even though you know they are wrong.

The Bible says that your words will prove whether or not you are guilty or innocent when you stand before God. Be sure that your speech reflects the part of you that you want to present to Jesus. Pray for His help as you work to keep your words clean and honorable to Him. He will honor your request by making wrongful words and speech ugly to you so that you won't even like hearing them, let alone saying them!

Whisper of Wisdom

"For it is by your words that you will not be guilty
and it is by your words that you will be guilty."

MATTHEW 12:37 NLV

Look What's Coming, Princess!

Wouldn't it be great if you didn't have to wait but you could see things change before your very eyes? Well, maybe someday!

You can't believe how long it takes to let your hair grow, but checking the mirror doesn't make it happen any faster. When you think things take too long, it's all the more exciting to hear that God will bring about the biggest change of all in an instant.

The Bible says that when Jesus comes again, at one look at Him you will become like Him. Amazing, isn't it, to realize that the biggest dream of all comes true with no waiting on your part. God can transform you in no time at all.

It's okay to steal a look in the mirror to see if your hair has grown. But when Jesus comes back, you'll be in for the surprise of your life. You won't even have time to wonder what's taking so long. The most phenomenal change of all will take place—you will be like Jesus. Awesome!

Whisper of Wisdom

We know that when he appears,
we shall be like him,
for we shall see him as he is.

1 JOHN 3:2 NIV

The Strength of the Lord

Are you weak? Fear not; God is strong.
He offers His strength to you.

Do you have a hard test or homework assignment coming up? Are you having some trouble making friends at your new school? Maybe things in your life are actually going very well, and you just want the comfort of Someone who is stronger than you.

Seek the Lord and His strength. When you recognize your own weaknesses and turn to Him, His strength will be made perfect in you.

He'll give you the ability to do your very best in school. He'll show you how to be a good friend so that you will attract nice friends. He'll wrap you in His love and lift you up so that you will properly handle every situation that comes your way.

Whisper of Wisdom

Seek the LORD and his strength,
seek his face continually.

1 CHRONICLES 16:11 KJV

I Demand My Rights

God's agreement with you is as simple as this: Trust in Him, accept the forgiveness gift of Jesus, and you're part of His family.

Have you ever felt cheated? Really and truly ripped off? Maybe you were overcharged for a purchase or you were skipped over when it was rightfully your turn to do something fun.

There are few guarantees in life. Plans fall through, circumstances change, and situations don't always turn out the way we planned.

The wonderful truth of God's kingdom is that His guarantee of everlasting life is airtight. The moment we repent of our sin and accept the grace Jesus secured by dying and rising again, God considers our names signed on the dotted line in His Book of Life. He hands us the keys to the kingdom, and our right to claim God as Father is set for eternity.

God is preparing a place for you in heaven this very moment. His plan for you to spend eternity with Him won't change. What are you doing on earth to prepare for your guaranteed future with Him?

Whisper of Wisdom

*To all who believed him and accepted him,
he gave the right to become children of God.*

JOHN 1:12 NLT

Keep On Keepin' On!

*Don't give up no matter how hard things get.
Keep on keepin' on, princess!*

Imagine you were asked to climb a mountain. Do you think you could make it to the top? What if you made it halfway but got tired? Would you turn around and climb back down, never to finish the journey?

Sometimes it's tempting to give up, especially when life gets hard. But your heavenly Father expects His daughters to keep on keepin' on. That means you keep going, even when things are tough!

Need an example? Maybe you're taking piano lessons, but things aren't going well. You can't seem to remember your scales, and your fingers get all mixed up when you try to play. Maybe everyone brags about your sister. (Her fingers seem to know what to do!) You practice and practice but don't seem to be improving. Wouldn't it make more sense to quit while you're ahead?

Of course not! Winners never quit—and quitters never win! So keep on practicing, princess! Before long, your fingers will fly across the keys!

Whisper of Wisdom

*You never saw him, yet you love him. You still
don't see him, yet you trust him—with laughter
and singing. Because you kept on believing, you'll
get what you're looking forward to: total salvation.*

1 PETER 1:8-9 MSG

Emotions

*Have you ever felt overwhelmed by your emotions?
It's okay to feel and express our emotions. It really is
natural to have emotional reactions to things in life.*

Our emotions can cause us problems when we feel we can't express them or talk them out with someone else. If we keep our emotions to ourselves, bottling them up inside, and cut ourselves off from others, we can end up alone and even physically ill.

We need each other to share the joy and the pain that come along with the adventures and challenges of living.

Jesus surrounded Himself with twelve close friends. Two of them, Peter and John, were His best of friends who shared His adventure on the Mount of Transfiguration, His fears in the Garden of Gethsemane, and the joys of His resurrection.

Find someone you can trust, someone you can share things with, and talk your emotions out.

Whisper of Wisdom

But as for me, I will sing of Your strength. Yes, I will sing with joy of Your loving-kindness in the morning. For You have been a strong and safe place for me in times of trouble.

PSALM 59:16 NLV

Rain, Rain, Go Away

What a gloomy day! Will the sun ever shine again?

Is a rain cloud hovering over your head? Everything seems to be going wrong and nobody understands. Are you sad and lonely? Do you feel like no one cares?

Life is full of gloomy days, when all you want to do is hide under the covers. But even though you may not feel Him, God is always there. He has promised He will never leave you alone. He can supply all of your needs. He cares when you have a rotten day. He sees your tears. He understands how you feel when no one else does. You are His own precious child, and more than anything, He wants you to be happy!

Pour out your heart to God. Tell Him all about what's troubling you. No one loves you more than your heavenly Father. And no one is better at calming the storms, chasing the clouds, and letting the sunshine in.

Whisper of Wisdom

Why am I discouraged? Why is my heart so sad? I will put my hope in God! I will praise him again—my Savior and my God!
PSALM 42:5-6 NLT

Stuck Like Glue

*Stick with what you've learned.
Don't let it slip away!*

*T*hink about all the things you've learned from your parents, Sunday school teachers, and the other adults in your life. They have a blast teaching you about the Bible, and you're a great student! God loves it when you remember what you've learned, but let's face it—it's easy to walk away and forget the lesson, isn't it?

Here's an example: You're in your Sunday school class and your teacher tells you all about the fruits of the Spirit. She explains that God wants you to be kind, good, gentle, faithful, and so on. You leave the class feeling really good about what you've learned. Then a few days later, you get in a fight with your little sister and treat her badly, forgetting all about the lesson.

Here's the problem with that: If we're going to be stuck like glue to what we've learned, we can't be patient one minute, then impatient the next. We can't be kind one minute, then mean the next. If the lesson really sticks, we have to go on doing the right thing, no matter what!

Ask God to help you live His Word, princess. And then before you know it, you'll be amazed at how well you can walk the talk.

Whisper of Wisdom

*Stick with what you learned and believed,
sure of the integrity of your teachers.*

2 TIMOTHY 3:14 MSG

Praising God in Song

*Have you listened to any music yet today? How about getting
in the habit of starting your day with a song for Him?*

The Bible mentions many different instruments, and it contains
numerous songs written in praise to God. David, the author of
many psalms, played the harp, and he played it so well that he was
summoned to play for King Saul when he was depressed or angry.

There are times when nothing but music will relax us or lift our
spirits. Whether it's on a stereo or an iPod, with friends or alone in our
room, music can take us to a place far away from our day-to-day life.

God created music not only for our enjoyment but also as a
means to praise Him. During your Bible study time, read through
some of the psalms—a collection of songs to God. Sing to Him a
worship chorus, or even compose a song for Him. He has given us
the gift of music; we can give back our gift of song.

Whisper of Wisdom

*Praise the Lord in song, for He has done excellent things;
let this be known throughout the earth.*

Isaiah 12:5 NASB

My Heart Is Right with God

Stay true to God.
Do not give up on your convictions.
Keep your heart pure.

God's Word is full of examples of people from whom you can learn many lessons about life. Spending time getting to know these individuals from the past will greatly enrich your life.

Take Job for example. What a wealthy, privileged man. He didn't take credit for his success, though. He walked humbly with God and gave Him all the glory. Yet with just a few words from Satan, God allowed Job's life to be turned upside down. Many people would have turned their backs on God, but not Job. Although he did question what was happening, he stayed true to the Lord. Then when his "friends" accused him of some sin that caused his suffering, Job was able to say with conviction, "My heart shall not reproach me."

Be true to God like Job was, and you, too, will maintain a clear conscience.

Whisper of Wisdom

My righteousness I hold fast, and will not let it go:
my heart shall not reproach me so long as I live.
JOB 27:6 KJV

Dedicated to the Princess

Don't you just love getting mail that's addressed to you?
It's not just for anybody—it's for you!

*D*o you try to find the "perfect" card or write a creative poem to express how special someone is to you? God, too, has His own way of telling you how wonderful you are, and it may not be what you'd guess.

The Bible says that God *sings* to you! He takes such great delight in you that He puts His thoughts to music. Wow, He creates a song just for you! You'd be excited enough to have your family or best friend call in to a radio station to dedicate a song to you. That would grab your attention, wouldn't it? But to think of the God of the universe, singing for you! How awesome is that?

Well, listen up when God announces that the next song is especially for you, His princess. You won't want to miss a word of it!

Whisper of Wisdom

"The LORD your God. . .will rejoice
over you with singing."
ZEPHANIAH 3:17 NIV

Pleasing God Is Easy. . .

We just need to follow His will and do what He asks. It's really not hard.

Did you ever want to please your parents or grandparents, so you did something you knew they wanted you to do—like walk the dog, clean your room, or be nice to your sister? Well, God wants you to please Him, too. But what can you do to please Him?

You will always please God by doing what's right. And God gave you the Bible so you'd know what "right" is. He also gave you parents and grandparents to help guide you.

You can also please God by loving mercy. He has shown us mercy by sending His Son to die for us. In turn, you can show mercy to others by being kind and forgiving them when they do you wrong.

Last but not least, please God by being humble—by not thinking you are better, or smarter, or prettier than others. It's that easy!

Remember all that God has done for you by pleasing Him. There's nothing to it!

Whisper of Wisdom

No, O people, the Lord has told you what is good, and this is what he requires of you: to do what is right, to love mercy, and to walk humbly with your God.

MICAH 6:8 NLT

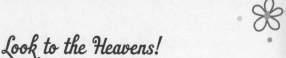

Look to the Heavens!

Sun and moon, twinkling stars, sing His praises from afar.

Have you ever gone outside at night and stared up at the stars? Did you notice how they twinkle against the dark sky—how they offer shimmers of light? Don't they look teensy-tiny up there, sparkling away?

The stars are actually huge! They're giant creations that only look small from earth! The stars. . .and the moon. . .and the sun. . .were placed in the sky by your heavenly Father. Why? Well, they serve a purpose, of course! But they're also there to show His glory, His majesty. If you close your eyes really tight (c'mon—close 'em!), you can almost imagine them singing the praises of God, telling the wonders of their awesome Creator.

The next time you look up into the sky and see a bright white star or a golden moon, pause a minute. Close your eyes. Think about God, seated on His throne in heaven—and seated on the throne of your heart. Doesn't just thinking about Him bring a huge smile to your face?

Well, what are you waiting for? Praise Him!

Whisper of Wisdom

The heavens declare the glory of God;
the skies proclaim the work of his hands.

Psalm 19:1 NIV

Troublemaker

Feeling too old to be told what to do?
Find out what God has to say about that!

Do you have a troublemaker in your class? Is someone you know always getting in trouble with the teacher? Hopefully that person isn't you! The Bible tells us that we should submit to our authorities and do good. Do you know what *submit* means? It means that you allow others to have authority over you and lead you—like your pastor and your parents and teachers.

Sometimes it's hard to always have people telling you what to do, but God wants us to follow the leaders He has put in our lives and not cause trouble for them. We have to trust that they know what is best for us.

Even as you grow older and become an adult, you will still have people in authority over you. Having a hard time with that? Ask God to help you submit to and honor everyone in your life who has leadership over you.

Whisper of Wisdom

Submit yourselves for the Lord's sake to every authority instituted among men. . . . For it is God's will that by doing good you should silence the ignorant talk of foolish men.

1 PETER 2:13, 15 NIV

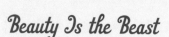

Beauty Is the Beast

When looks are all we think about, appearance becomes a beast.

Esther was a girl not much older than you. She lived in 465 BC in the area that is now Pakistan.

The ruler of Esther's land, King Xerxes (pronounced "Zerksees"), wanted to find a new queen. So he sent servants throughout the land to find the prettiest girls and bring them to the palace for a beauty pageant. The winner, chosen by the king, would be the new queen.

Esther was chosen as a contestant. The king valued beauty so much, he proclaimed that each contestant would receive a year of beauty treatments with oils, perfumes, and makeup to make them gorgeous. *A whole year!*

When we focus on making our outsides beautiful, we forget to work on our inner beauty–kindness, gentleness, faithfulness, and, most important, our faith in God. Trying to have the prettiest face, nicest hair, and coolest clothes smothers our desire to please God, who values inner beauty above all.

How did Esther's story end? Esther loved God and depended on His strength and guidance. After she became queen, she risked her life to save her people. Esther was truly beautiful on the inside as well as the outside.

Whisper of Wisdom

You give me strength and guide me right.
PSALM 18:32 CEV

Nothing but the Truth

It's just a harmless little fib.
It won't hurt anyone. Right?

Wrong!

The Bible tells us that God *hates* lies. Why? Because they hurt so many people. Remember Adam and Eve? When they listened to the serpent's guile and disobeyed God, their happy life was over forever.

Lies are tricky and sly. They pretend to be harmless and even necessary at times. They give themselves names like "Fib" and "Tale" and paint themselves white to try to fool you into using them. And once you give in and tell one, you're trapped. The lie will cling to you, growing bigger and bigger until you can't hide it anymore. Soon everyone will see its ugly head sticking out.

Lies destroy trust. Once you've been caught being dishonest, it will be harder for others to believe you, even when you *do* tell the truth. Your reputation for integrity will be tarnished, and it'll take a long time to shine it up again.

Because you are a daughter of the heavenly King, lies do not become you. Don't be fooled by lies and their crafty, evil ways. Be open and honest, telling the truth at all times.

Whisper of Wisdom

"But this is what you must do:
Tell the truth to each other."
ZECHARIAH 8:16 NLT

The Place to Be

*To strike up a conversation in a group,
find out something you all have in common.*

If you're in the mood to do girl talk, you get with a bunch of girlfriends. If you want to brag about your pet dog, you'll want a dog-lovers' audience. So whom does God's princess seek out when she wants to share the cool things God is doing in her life?

Naturally, says the psalmist, you go to others who love "God talk," like your Sunday school class, family, or good friends. They want to hear how God is helping you to, say, sleep soundly without scary dreams, keep calm when the class bully comes around, or talk to a neighbor about Jesus. Not only will their support give you a faith boost, but God will use your words to encourage them.

God loves to hear His family brag about Him! Even if you need to hunt for other "God lovers," insist on having "God talk." You'll find out you have a lot in common.

Whisper of Wisdom

I will proclaim your name to my brothers and sisters.
PSALM 22:22 NLT

Friends Share Everything

*What makes a friend a friend? You're in Jesus'
circle of friends when you hear what He has to say.*

Who are your friends? Classmates? Kids at church? Maybe you have one or two friends who are extra special—friends you can tell anything. There's Someone else who has named you as a friend since the beginning of time. He knows everything about you—from your love of string cheese to your habit of twirling your hair around your finger—and He loves you no matter what. That friend is Jesus.

For the years Jesus lived on earth, He told His followers many seemingly crazy things, like "I'm going to allow other people to kill Me—to take My life. But after three days I will come to life again to fulfill God's plan." He taught about forgiveness, about loving others, about compassion, and about the consequences of not following after Him.

He wants you to take full advantage of the friendship He offers by sharing your life with Him. That means telling Him about your worries and disappointments and sharing your happiness and accomplishments through praise.

Whisper of Wisdom

*"I've named you friends because I've let you in
on everything I've heard from the Father."*

JOHN 15:15 MSG

Tutti-Frutti

Good fruit, bad fruit,
Happy fruit, sad fruit.

Did you know that people recognize you by your fruit? No, we're not talking about apples and oranges here. We're talking about the fruits of the Spirit: love, joy, peace, patience, kindness, and so on. If you stick close to Jesus (like vines clinging to the branch of a tree), you will bear good fruit, but if you wander far away, you will bear bad fruit.

Nothing is more disgusting than rotten old fruit. Ever eat a brown, squishy banana? How about a dried-up orange? Ever had a mushy strawberry or a moldy peach? Gross, right?

Here's the thing: When people look at you, they see either good fruit or bad fruit. Either they see love, joy, and patience, or they see someone who's grumpy, hard to get along with, and impatient! They see either someone who has a helpful attitude or someone who always wants to get her own way.

So which is it, daughter of the King? Good fruit? Bad fruit? Happy fruit? Or sad fruit? The decision is up to you.

Whisper of Wisdom

"Make a tree good and its fruit will be good,
or make a tree bad and its fruit will be bad,
for a tree is recognized by its fruit."

MATTHEW 12:33 NIV

It's Not My Problem!

Sometimes you just want to shout out, "It's not my problem! Why should I help? It has nothing to do with me!"

We all have troubles from time to time. Turning a book report in late. Missing the school bus. Losing homework. Arguing with brothers and sisters. Disagreeing with Mom and Dad.

How do you feel when you have troubles of your own? Lonely? Helpless? Afraid? Worried? You probably have at least one if not all of those feelings. Now imagine what you would do if you had no one to talk to. . .no one to help you through a tough time. Handling your problems all by yourself would make your troubles seem even bigger, wouldn't it?

Even though we may want to turn and run away from someone else's problems, we are called to follow God's example and reach out to help others in their time of need. Whether they need a listening ear, a shoulder to cry on, or an extra set of hands to complete a big chore, we can pitch in and let God's light shine through us.

Whisper of Wisdom

Help each other in troubles and problems.
This is the kind of law Christ asks us to obey.

GALATIANS 6:2 NLV

Sacrifice of Praise

Awake with a song on your lips.
Praise God throughout the day.
Lie down with a joyful heart.

When you wake up for school, do you grumble, or do you praise God for a new day to serve Him? Do you whine because your mom fixes scrambled eggs instead of French toast, or are you genuinely grateful for whatever is put before you?

Did you know that we are continually to praise and thank God for who He is and all He has done for us? That means you thank God for the math test as well as the snow day. You thank Him when your brother takes a shower at night and when he hogs the bathroom in the morning when you're trying to get ready.

Praising God is a command, but it's also a special privilege. When our hearts are filled with thankfulness to our Creator, it leads to a true sense of peace and joy deep within.

Whisper of Wisdom

By him therefore let us offer the sacrifice
of praise to God continually, that is, the fruit
of our lips giving thanks to his name.
HEBREWS 13:15 KJV

Forgiveness

It's important for a Christian to be able to let go of anger toward others and extend forgiveness to them, just as Jesus offers forgiveness to us.

Forgiveness is one of the most basic Christian principles. Without forgiveness, there would be no salvation. Without salvation, there would be no eternity in heaven. Does Jesus hold a grudge against you for the things you've done wrong? No! He tells us that if we simply confess those things to Him, then He will forgive us and make us clean of all our wrongdoings. The Bible also says that He doesn't even remember what we did.

Because of the forgiveness that Jesus has given so freely to us, He expects us to forgive others. Jesus wants us to forgive people when they do wrong to us. So when someone wrongs you, even before they apologize, ask Him to help you forgive them. By freely offering forgiveness and mercy to those who hurt you, you are being an example of Jesus' love.

Whisper of Wisdom

If we confess our sins, He is faithful and just to forgive us our sins and to cleanse us from all unrighteousness.

1 John 1:9 NKJV

The Princess Cooler

Have you seen beautiful petunias that start to droop and wilt?
Run and grab the watering can.

There's nothing like a chilled glass of lemonade after helping your mom plant flowers on a hot summer day. Now that you're refreshed, you can get up and go again. Did you know that God's princess can refresh others in God's family with "cool" words and "cool" actions?

You mean a "cooler" is a picker-upper? Listen to this! The original apostles didn't know if Saul, who later became Paul, followed Jesus like they did. Think how Saul felt when they didn't trust him, but along came Barnabas. He stood with Saul and said that he *really did* come to know Jesus on the road to Damascus. What a refresher! In fact, Barnabas's "cool" words and actions refreshed the whole church (Acts 9:26–31).

Do you know a princess in need of a "cooler"? She may not be too hot from the sun, but she may be famished for friendship. Are you ready to pour a glass of lemonade?

Whisper of Wisdom

Your kindness has often refreshed
the hearts of God's people.

PHILEMON 7 NLT

"Oh, Be Careful, Little Eyes. . ."

*Remember the song "Oh, Be Careful, Little Eyes"
from early Sunday school days? Are we careful in
choosing to look only at things that please Jesus?*

The Bible tells us, "If your eye causes you to sin, gouge it out and throw it away." This paints a picture that would most likely get the response, "Ewww!" Yet Jesus wanted to get our attention, to let us know how important it is to keep our eyes from viewing things that are sinful.

There are many things for our eyes to view: TV, the Internet, movies, magazines. . . Just as there are numerous things to look at that would please Jesus, there are countless things that would not please Him. We must use wisdom in choosing the things we view.

God made our eyes, and He desires that we use them for His glory. Decide to make good choices in what you look at today. Start by reading the Bible, because the closer your relationship with Jesus, the easier it will be to make the right choice.

Whisper of Wisdom

*"If your eye causes you to sin,
gouge it out and throw it away."*
MATTHEW 18:9 NLT

Be Like Jesus

You might wear the latest styles, or last year's outfits might do, but the righteousness of Jesus is the best garment of all.

It's human nature to want the best of everything. Sometimes it goes beyond desire and becomes the dreaded enemy. Your friend gets the new bike you've been wanting, and suddenly you're so jealous of her that you refuse to speak to her.

"She always gets whatever she wants," you grumble. You are so consumed with jealousy that your friendship turns sour. You are letting greed control you.

It should be Christ who controls your desires. If you let Him clothe you in His righteousness, there will be no room for lusts of the flesh. Remember how Satan tempted Jesus with several things? Jesus knew scripture so well that He was able to turn from temptation. You have His Word, too. Get to know it. Satan and his worldly offers don't stand a chance against the Bible.

Whisper of Wisdom

But put ye on the Lord Jesus Christ, and make not provision for the flesh, to fulfil the lusts thereof.

ROMANS 13:14 KJV

Salty Christians

Just a pinch goes a long, long way!

Imagine you're at a fast-food place and have just ordered a cheeseburger and french fries. You taste the fries, only to discover there's no salt on them. In fact, you can't find salt anywhere in the restaurant. Sure, you go ahead and eat the fries, but they're not very tasty, are they? And it's not like you need a lot of salt to fix the problem. Just a little bit would be enough.

That's how it is when you share your faith with people who don't know the Lord. Just a pinch here and there goes a long, long way. They don't need you to preach to them. (Talk about overloading the salt!) They just need little sprinkles, enough to make them thirsty for the Gospel.

That's our job, after all—to make people thirsty for the Lord. He calls us to reach others for Him. What an adventure! So grab that saltshaker, princess! God has work for you to do!

Whisper of Wisdom

"You are the salt of the earth. But if the salt loses its saltiness, how can it be made salty again? It is no longer good for anything, except to be thrown out and trampled by men."

MATTHEW 5:13 NIV

No Revenge

When someone treats you badly, you may be tempted
to get even—but is that what God wants you to do?

Did you ever have someone you thought you could trust give away a secret? You may have wanted to teach her a lesson by doing the same to her. Or how about when someone pushed you? Did you ever feel like pushing him right back?

It's not hard to want to treat others the same way they treat you. But God wants you to love them even when they don't seem lovable.

But here's what's so cool. When you treat others the way God wants you to—by loving them, doing good to them, and praying for them no matter what—you will be much happier with yourself. And you may be very surprised by the change of heart they might have because of your kindness toward them.

Whisper of Wisdom

"But I say to you, love your enemies, bless those who curse you, do good to those who hate you, and pray for those who spitefully use you and persecute you."

MATTHEW 5:44 NKJV

The Whole Puzzle

God sees the picture of your life as it's meant to be.
Trust Him to help you put the pieces together according to His will.

Have you ever tried to assemble a jigsaw puzzle without having the picture on the front of the box? It's not easy. You may have a thousand pieces that somehow fit together to make a beautiful portrait, but without the whole picture, they look like nothing more than a mess of colors.

Our lives on earth are something like that. We cry out to God, asking for His help to make sense of the jumble of problem pieces we have on earth that we can't sort out. God is the only One who owns the finished picture. He sees how the happiness and trouble in our lives fit together in the end.

He answers our prayers, telling us to give our burdens to Him. He helps us work them out, arranging the pieces of our puzzles in a way that will make the picture full and complete in the end. We won't always understand why He's doing what He's doing, so He asks us to follow Him in faith.

What trouble pieces do you have in your life? Ask God to take care of those problems by placing them in the right spot so they will ultimately work together for good.

Whisper of Wisdom

And we know that in all things God works
for the good of those who love him,
who have been called according to his purpose.
ROMANS 8:28 NIV

A Princess Perspective

Does time really go faster on weekends?
Maybe it's because you get to do some of your favorite things.

Twenty seconds without laughing may drag if you're one who likes to giggle. Time goes too fast, though, when you get to read a mystery thriller. Just another page, you say. God hopes His princess thinks that all the time in the world wouldn't be long enough to praise Him.

That's why David, when he led the Israelites in worship, thought he'd run out of time before he ran out of reasons to praise God. He was caught up in praising God as he watched the people bring their offerings to build the temple. David concluded it would take forever and ever to praise God in every way He deserves.

The next time you gasp at what God has done for you, turn away from the clock and start telling God how great He is. When you check, you may be surprised to see what time it is!

Whisper of Wisdom

"May You be praised, Lord God. . .
from eternity to eternity."
1 Chronicles 29:10 hcsb

Nobody's Perfect!

Loving someone means not holding grudges.

How could you go in my room when I'm not here and take my things without asking?" Alyssa asked her younger sister, Emily. "You knew it was wrong, but you did it anyway!"

"Come on, Alyssa, I would have asked if you were home. I needed a clean soccer jersey for the match today, and all of mine were dirty. Can't you just forgive and forget? You would have done the same thing."

"No, I wouldn't! I treat your things as *your things* and ask out of respect if I need to borrow something. What you did was actually stealing."

"I'm really sorry, Alyssa. I was wrong, and I promise never to do it again."

Alyssa could feel her anger ebbing away. She knew Emily had meant no harm. "Why were all your jerseys dirty, anyway?"

Emily hung her head. "I forgot to put them in the hamper for Mom on wash day, and I don't know how to do laundry."

Alyssa smiled at her kid sister. "It's a good thing I love you, or I'd be turning you in to the clothes police! Now I'm going to teach you how to sling a little laundry detergent!"

Whisper of Wisdom

Love overlooks the wrongs that others do.
PROVERBS 10:12 CEV

Liar, Liar

*Are you a truth teller. . .
or are your pants on fire?*

You've heard the little taunt "Liar, liar, pants on fire." You may have even said it a time or two. Does it apply to you? Are you in the habit of telling lies? Not *huge* lies. . .but those little white lies that don't seem to make much of a difference? You know—telling Mom you finished all of your homework when you really have two more problems to solve, or telling your best friend that a certain boy likes her just to make her feel good when you don't know that for sure? You get the idea.

The Bible is crystal clear on lying: God hates it! Even the little white lies that are meant to make others feel good. If you are really curious, look up Revelation 21:8. It describes what happens to people who make a lifelong habit of lying. Yikes! Ask God to help you be truthful in everything you say and do.

Whisper of Wisdom

*The Lord detests lying lips,
but he delights in those who tell the truth.*

Proverbs 12:22 NLT

Behaving Wisely

You are maturing so quickly. Are you determined to walk wisely? Why not let others see God in you?

You know the story of young David. He had proven he was responsible enough to care for his father's sheep. When wild beasts attacked, he showed wisdom in the way he protected the sheep. When he was given the task of carrying food to his soldier brothers, he probably didn't anticipate that God would use him to win an important victory, but he was prepared when it happened. While David was still young, God called upon David, who had already served as King Saul's musician, to be the next king of Israel.

Why was God able to use David this way? It's simple, really. David had determined to live wisely and maturely. He chose this path when he was a child, and you can choose it, too. You can decide that with God's strength, you will walk perfectly. Then others will trust you, and God will use you in a special way!

Whisper of Wisdom

I will behave myself wisely in a perfect way.
O when wilt thou come unto me?
I will walk within my house with a perfect heart.

PSALM 101:2 KJV

Leader of the Pack

R-E-S-P-E-C-T. Find out what it means to lead.

*H*ave you ever thought about the word *respect*? Do you know what it means to respect your elders (those who are older than you)? Think about the adults you know—your parents, grandparents, and church leaders. Do you realize God has placed them in your life for a reason? And He's watching you closely to make sure you treat them with the respect they deserve.

Imagine this: A leader at your church (maybe your Sunday school teacher or children's church pastor) isn't getting a lot of respect from the kids in the class. Maybe some of your friends are talking when they should be listening, or interrupting when the teacher is speaking. What can you do to help? By far the best thing you can do is treat the teacher with respect. Then encourage others to do the same. Don't be part of the problem—be part of the solution. The teacher will be grateful, and pretty soon all of the kids will follow your lead.

So why treat your leaders with respect? Because it's the right thing to do!

Whisper of Wisdom

Dear brothers and sisters, honor those who are your leaders in the Lord's work. They work hard among you and give you spiritual guidance.

1 Thessalonians 5:12 NLT

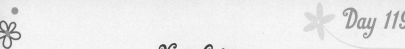

Keep Going

When life is tough, it's hard to have a good attitude. But God gives guidance to get through it: Be joyful, keep praying, and give thanks.

Everyone struggles with having a bad attitude sometimes. Maybe it only takes one bad thing to spoil your mood for a whole day. It may seem impossible to improve your attitude once you start feeling upset, but God says there's another way.

Pray. Choose to be joyful. Find ways to be thankful for what's happening in your life. This is what God wants His children to do every day, no matter how difficult life is. Sound challenging?

You may have to start out small. When you feel like your attitude is slipping, take a moment to pray and ask God to help change your outlook. Thank Him for something that is important to you. Then practice joy. Take these God-directed steps, and He'll help pull your attitude out of the dumps.

God doesn't want you to go through life with a sour attitude. Choose today to live with the outlook of Christ, and He'll give you the strength to make it through.

Whisper of Wisdom

Always be joyful. Never stop praying.
Be thankful in all circumstances, for this is
God's will for you who belong to Christ Jesus.

1 THESSALONIANS 5:16-18 NLT

What's the Princess Cooking Up?

*Even if you don't help fix the meal, stir up tasty treats anyway.
They'll make a hit with everyone.*

You love placing your order if your family goes out to eat, while at home you might not get to pick what's *on* the table. You can still select, princess, what to bring *to* the table.

Bring with you a pleasant look for each one around the table instead of rolling your eyes at a pesky younger sibling. Add to that genuine thanks to Mom or whoever prepared the meal. Like sour grapes, gripes don't sit very well with anyone. Toss in a little humor, too. It helps the food to digest, while crude remarks cause heartburn. Top off your tasty treats with a compliment. Remember, flattery is a little too sugary.

So before you ask what's for dinner, stir up princess-style treats. God would be honored to join you at the table.

Whisper of Wisdom

*Better a dry crust eaten in peace than a
house filled with feasting—and conflict.*

PROVERBS 17:1 NLT

Hidden Treasures

*Take three steps to the east, two to the north. . .
Now open your eyes, and stay on course!*

Imagine a map of a deserted island, one that would lead you to the greatest buried treasure ever found. You follow the map until you come across a chest filled with priceless gold coins. What would you do with all that money? Go to the mall? Spread the joy by taking your friends out for ice cream? Help your parents pay the bills?

The Bible says that the kingdom of heaven is like a treasure hidden in a field. It is a thing of great value. When you come into a relationship with Jesus, you've discovered the greatest treasure of all—one that will lead you all the way to heaven one day. The Christian life is a priceless gift, one you can't take for granted.

And guess what—God wants you to share that gift with others. Leave clear directions for others to follow so that they, too, will one day discover this awesome treasure!

Whisper of Wisdom

*"The kingdom of heaven is like treasure hidden in a field.
When a man found it, he hid it again, and then in his
joy went and sold all he had and bought that field."*

MATTHEW 13:44 NIV

Day 122

Breakfast of Champions

Want to start your day off right? Take some time to eat!

What do you have for breakfast? A bowl of cereal? Pancakes with syrup? Eggs and toast? Whatever it is, chances are that you don't start your day without putting something in your stomach. But how many times have you headed off to school without feeding your soul?

As a child of God, you face a lot of challenges. Choosing between right and wrong, fighting temptation, and dealing with difficult people all take spiritual muscles. The best way to build those muscles is by feeding on a steady diet of God's Word. Reading the Bible is like giving your soul a big stack of pancakes. It provides the spiritual energy you need to make it through the day.

Start your morning with God. Instead of reading the back of the cereal box, read a few passages from the Bible. Then take a moment to pray and ask God to help you with whatever you might face. That's the breakfast of a champion! And what an amazing difference a well-fed soul can make.

Whisper of Wisdom

Man doth not live by bread only, but by every word that proceedeth out of the mouth of the LORD.
DEUTERONOMY 8:3 KJV

No Worries

Don't waste time worrying about tomorrow
when you have things to take care of today.

Amy was so worried about the test she had to take the next day that she wasn't paying attention to what her teacher was saying. She tried to think about all she'd need to study that evening. She needed to go back over all her tests and make sure she knew the answers to the questions she got wrong. She needed. . .

"Okay, class, I've given you fifteen minutes. Put your books up; it's quiz time," Mr. O' Bryant said.

"Quiz time?" Amy whispered to her friend Beth.

"You didn't hear what he said? If we ace this quiz, we don't have to take the test tomorrow."

Amy groaned. She hadn't been paying attention. She panicked as her teacher laid a sheet of paper on her desk. She was so nervous she couldn't think. She failed the quiz by two points. If she'd just listened instead of worrying about tomorrow, she wouldn't have had to take tomorrow's test! She wasn't going to waste time worrying about the next day anymore—today held its own set of problems!

Whisper of Wisdom

"Don't worry about tomorrow, for tomorrow will bring its own worries. Today's trouble is enough for today."

Matthew 6:34 NLT

Outrun Your Shadow

The influence you have on others cannot be avoided any more than you can remove a shadow on a sunny day.

Have you ever tried to outrun your shadow? It would obviously be an impossible thing to do. The influence you have on others is much like that shadow. No matter how you try, it doesn't go away. You are accountable for what your words and actions lead others to think about Jesus. Your behavior has a direct impact on the thoughts and the salvation of the people around you.

What kind of influence do you have? Are you kind, honest, and faithful? Do you live in a way that would cause unsaved people to want to know Jesus?

Princesses of the kingdom should influence other kingdom dwellers to live for Jesus, too. Do you have that kind of influence?

Being out under the bright sun gives you a good, sharp shadow. Living close to the Son of God helps you build a good, strong Christian influence.

Whisper of Wisdom

*As he who called you is holy,
you also be holy in all your conduct.*

1 Peter 1:15 esv

20/20 Vision

*Are you seeing clearly? If your eyes are on Jesus,
He helps you see everything with 20/20 vision!*

Have you had your eyesight tested this year at school? Do you have perfect vision, or are your eyes a little fuzzy and in need of some help from your glasses? Glasses or no glasses, God's Word tells us to fix our eyes on Jesus. That's the only way we are clearly able to see how to live a godly life every day.

When our eyes are fixed on Jesus, we are able to see the good in every situation. We are able to see what needs fixing in our own life. We are able to see the truth. . .clearly! Where are your eyes fixed? Do you often see the negative side of things? Are you looking at the waves instead of the One who calms the storms? Fix your eyes on Jesus, and ask Him to clear up your "heavenly vision"!

Whisper of Wisdom

*Let us fix our eyes on Jesus,
the author and perfecter of our faith.*

HEBREWS 12:2 NIV

Faithful in Tasks

In your work, do you think, Do I have to?
Or is it, No big deal; I can do that!

If you haven't already done some kind of task yet today, it's probably just a matter of time until you have to. Are you responsible for filling the dishwasher? Taking out the trash? Cleaning the bathroom?

Some chores aren't too difficult to complete. They can be done with a fairly good attitude. But other tasks, well, there's just no way to keep a good attitude while completing them. . .or is there?

When Adam and Eve were sent away from the Garden of Eden, God declared that hard work would be necessary from then on. Proverbs tells us that if we want reward or success, we must work; but the Bible also tells us to have a good attitude in all we do.

So since we have to work, we may as well make it as enjoyable as possible. Listen to your favorite music. Take the time to daydream. And complete that task as if the Lord Himself asked you to do it.

Whisper of Wisdom

To enjoy your work and accept your lot in life—
this is indeed a gift from God.

ECCLESIASTES 5:19 NLT

Don't Give Up

*You're not complete yet—God's still working on you.
And He won't stop until He's finished.*

Have you ever started a hobby, an instrument, a sports team—only to get bored or find out it's too hard and give up a short time later? Maybe you're an expert channel surfer, clicking through TV stations with lightning speed to try to find something better to watch.

God knows we have short attention spans. He also assures us that's one characteristic we don't share with the Creator. When God starts something, He sees it through. Creation of the heavens and earth—check, check. Creation of humans—check. Birth, life, death, and resurrection of Jesus—check, check, check, check. Defeat of Satan—check.

God's follow-through is great news for Christians. God began His work in you the moment He thought you into existence. His project continued when you first heard about Him. He continued His work as you accepted Christ and became a Christian, and He'll continue working on you until you walk through the gates of heaven.

God doesn't get bored with you. He never will. Thank Him for His special attention to and continued work in your life.

Whisper of Wisdom

*God is the one who began this good work in you,
and I am certain that he won't stop before it is
complete on the day that Christ Jesus returns.*

PHILIPPIANS 1:6 CEV

Graceful Feet

*God's princess might wish to step on a wad of
bubble gum—any excuse to stall the next move.*

If you have to do something for the first time ever, do you bite a
fingernail or feel butterflies in your stomach? When you head in a
new direction, remember that God will help you put one foot in front
of the other.

With every step that follows, God will give you courage just as
He gave courage to a young woman in Bible times. Perhaps Ruth
hesitated to leave her home, but God had already helped her walk
away from false gods and follow Him. If God could do that, then He'd
give her courage to head out to a new place to live.

If your family moves, God will help you walk through the door of
a brand-new school or step out into a new neighborhood. If you're
tempted to drag your feet or stop in your tracks, ask God to help you,
His princess, take a graceful step in the right direction.

Whisper of Wisdom

*"Be strong and courageous. . .for the LORD
your God is with you wherever you go."*

JOSHUA 1:9 HCSB

Lies Aren't Little or White

There's no way around it: Lies are lies.

"I never said I'd do *everything* with her!" Caitlyn, her hands defiantly on her hips, faced her friend Adrienne.

"No, but you told Jenna you'd help her find a dress for her piano recital after school. She's depending on you," Adrienne said.

"But I didn't know I'd get invited to sit with the pep squad at the game!"

"Caitlyn, Jenna's recital is Saturday. Friday's your last chance to help her."

"I know," Caitlyn admitted, "but I *really* want to go to the game. I'll say Mrs. Mitchell asked me to stay after school to help decorate for the Fall Festival."

"But that's a lie."

"It's only a little white lie. She did ask me to decorate—from three thirty until four. Jenna doesn't have to know the game starts at four."

Adrienne shook her head. "Half an apple is still an apple. Half a lie is still a lie. Do you really think God thinks a *little* lie is okay?"

"No, I guess not. Okay. You're right." Caitlyn smiled. "I'd feel like the worm in that apple if I didn't keep my word."

Whisper of Wisdom

Never tell lies or be deceitful in what you say.
Proverbs 4:24 cev

Pure Joy!

Think about all the lovely things God has given for your enjoyment—not just "stuff," but the things in life that really matter. He has blessed you with so much that you could have an "I've been blessed" celebration every day of the week!

Think about some things you'd like to have.... Pretty easy, right? Maybe you've been wanting a new pair of jeans or shoes. Or maybe you'd like to have a brand-new stereo in your room. We always have a ready list of "stuff" that would make us just a little happier, don't we?

But have you ever made a list—an A-to-Z, everything-that's-good-in-your-life list? From the simple to the big stuff—sunshine, your favorite food, your lovable (only occasionally annoying) sister or brother, your friends, your bike, your house, your favorite family vacation spot—you have too many blessings to name!

While we often tend to think about all of the things we don't have, the fact is that every moment of the day, no matter where you look, you can find at least one item to thank God for—one blessing in your life. Now that's reason to celebrate. . .all day long!

Whisper of Wisdom

Celebrate God all day, every day.
PHILIPPIANS 4:4 MSG

Conceit-o-Meter

Me? Stuck-up? Impossible!

Some girls take the princess thing a bit too far. C'mon! You know it happens. Girls—even Christian girls—sometimes act a little, well. . .stuck-up. They think they're "all that" (better than the others in their group). Maybe you've met girls like that. Maybe you've been a girl like that.

The problem with thinking you're better than others is that the Bible teaches us to do exactly the opposite—to think of others as better than ourselves. It's true! And if we're only focused on ourselves (our clothes, hair, popularity, and so forth), we're not really thinking of others, are we?

Today's verse shows us that we're not supposed to do anything out of conceit. That means we can't brag about ourselves. We can't go around putting others down to make ourselves look better. (Oh, I know it's tempting!) We have to remember that God wants us to put others first. (Sound impossible? It's not!) We just have to lay down our selfishness and love them the way He loves them—and us!

Whisper of Wisdom

*Do nothing out of selfish ambition or vain conceit,
but in humility consider others better than yourselves.*

PHILIPPIANS 2:3 NIV

Something about That Name

It's important to respect God's name.

"Oh my God!" Loren exclaimed, turning to her friend Kari. "Can you believe the color of this nail polish? My toes look like they're covered in grape jelly!"

Kari looked at her friend in surprise. "Why would you pray about that?"

"Pray?" Loren looked puzzled. "What do you mean?"

"You just called on the name of God. My youth director says every time we use God's name, we're praying. The Bible says *whenever* we call on God's name, He hears us. We should only use God's name when we want His attention. It's like a loudspeaker to heaven."

"Really?" Loren glanced at her feet. "I sure didn't mean to drag God away from something important. . .over my toenails. I guess now that I think about it, God wouldn't be very happy about the number of times each day I call His name over dumb stuff."

"Yeah," Kari agreed. "Remember the story about the boy who cried 'Wolf!' for fun too many times, and when he *really* needed help, nobody believed him? I don't want to 'dis' the name of God so that when I'm seriously praying—"

"He'll seriously answer," Loren said, finishing Kari's sentence.

Whisper of Wisdom

"Call to Me and I will answer you."
JEREMIAH 33:3 NASB

Always with Thanksgiving

Be thankful for the blessings and gifts in your life.
Show your gratitude by being satisfied and not
always longing for the "better" thing.

When we receive a gift, we gratefully unwrap it and then show real appreciation for the gift. We wouldn't dream of not offering thanks for the gifts we are given. Often the gift isn't even something that we wanted or asked for. But the giver thought it suited us or believed we would put it to good use. Most important, the gift giver took time, thought, and money to select the gift and then took great care in presenting it.

How much more does our heavenly Father take care in choosing the gifts that He gives to us? Jesus wants us not only to be satisfied with what we have, but to be grateful for it. His desire is that we live with gratitude for all of our blessings and not with selfishness, which always demands more. He will give us all we need, and He will never leave us wanting for more, if we desire His will.

Whisper of Wisdom

Don't fall in love with money. Be satisfied with what you have.
The Lord has promised that he will not leave us or desert us.

Hebrews 13:5 cev

Friends Who Love God

Who are your friends? Do they honor and respect God?
Do they follow God's commands?

Friends are special people in your life, and you are going to value their opinions. You will also pick up on their attitudes and values. That's why it is so important to choose friends who put God first in their lives. You want your closest companions to be those who recognize the importance of obeying God's commands.

Positive, godly peer pressure is a good thing. It is a blessing to be around people who encourage you to follow God's Word. In turn, you can also set the example of recognizing who God is and obeying Him. You just can't go wrong when you determine to have friends who love and obey the Lord. Surround yourself with them. Don't fall into the trap of wanting to be with the "in" crowd. Choose to be different. Choose to love God.

Whisper of Wisdom

I am a companion of all them that fear thee,
and of them that keep thy precepts.
PSALM 119:63 KJV

"Did You Hear. . . ?"

*Spreading gossip can hurt others' feelings and ruin a friendship.
That's a high price to pay for just a few words!*

Have you ever said something about someone behind her back?
That might not be too easy to remember. But you can most likely
think of a time you found out that someone said something about
you behind *your* back. How did you feel? Probably not too great,
especially since you can *still* remember it!

Get in the habit of taking a moment to think of the words that
are ready to come out of your mouth. If they will harm someone,
keep them inside—don't speak them. That can be extremely difficult,
especially if someone has hurt *your* feelings. But God commands us
to control our tongue so that we don't dishonor Him or hurt those He
has created.

If you control your tongue, you will be an example who will point
others toward Jesus—and you will save a friendship, too!

Whisper of Wisdom

*Don't talk about your neighbors behind their backs—no slander
or gossip, please. Don't say to anyone, "I'll get back at you for
what you did to me. I'll make you pay for what you did!"*

PROVERBS 24:28 MSG

Warning: Do Not Lift!

Some things are too heavy for a princess to pick up.
Why bother?

Carrying a bag of groceries into the house? No problem. Toting your luggage to visit grandparents? You can handle it. Hmm, better not try the Empire State Building! God warns His princess, too, that some things are just too heavy, like trying to hold on to a grudge. Now *that's* heavy!

Of all people, Joseph, a man in the Old Testament, had every reason to hold a grudge against his brothers. They were incredibly mean to him. How tempting to get even. Like Joseph, remember that vengeance belongs to God. If you rest your case with Him, He is even able to turn someone's harm into good (Genesis 50:20). Imagine that!

Staying grudge-free allows you to load up on loving deeds like Joseph did for his brothers—and loving deeds are much lighter than a grudge. Want to heap these kindnesses on those who hurt you? Just ask Joseph how freeing it feels!

Whisper of Wisdom

"Do not seek revenge or bear a grudge. . .
but love your neighbor as yourself.
I am the LORD."
LEVITICUS 19:18 NIV

BFF
(Best Friend Forever)

A best friend is someone we trust with our dreams and our fears, someone we depend on as we go through life's tough times.

Becky and Jamie were BFFs all through elementary school until Jamie moved away and they lost touch. Keira and Nicole were BFFs until middle school when their likes and dislikes started to change and they made new friends with the same new interests.

Losing a BFF can be a sad, painful process, but as we grow older, change is a part of life that we can't avoid. But if we've asked Jesus to be our BFF, then we can count on Him never to move away and never change His interest in us and what is important to us.

Jesus has promised us that what He says is true and that He will always be there for us. So even though things around us in life must change, we can count on Jesus to be our true BFF.

Whisper of Wisdom

*The grass dries up. The flower loses its color.
But the Word of our God stands forever.*
ISAIAH 40:8 NLV

I Belong to God

Your body is home to God's Spirit. He wants you to
treat your body in a way that honors the Creator.

Sydney acted differently when her parents weren't around.

Alone with her friends, Sydney sometimes let a bad word or two escape from her mouth. She'd wear extra makeup and not worry if a little skin showed when her shirt and pants didn't quite meet in the middle. She flirted with boys—a lot—and didn't care what anyone thought of her.

But when her mom and dad were nearby, Sydney became a different person. She sat up straighter, spoke only kind words, wiped some of her dark eye makeup off, pulled her shirt down to cover up, and smiled politely at boys.

Sometimes we live two lives—one for God and one for ourselves. Maybe Sunday is the day of the week when we sit up straight and think good thoughts about Jesus and the Bible, but Monday through Saturday we slouch and think only about ourselves.

The truth is that God's Spirit lives inside of Christians every day of the week. Honor Him today by realizing your body is home for your heavenly Father—then let your actions follow.

Whisper of Wisdom

Don't you realize that your body is the temple of the
Holy Spirit, who lives in you and was given to you by God?
You do not belong to yourself, for God bought you with
a high price. So you must honor God with your body.

1 Corinthians 6:19-20 NLT

No Fear

*When fear grips you,
look to the Lord for help.*

What do you do when you're faced with the unknown or have to do something you're afraid of—like starting a new school and meeting new people, or getting up and speaking in front of the class? Where can you turn?

Turn to God. Take a deep breath and remember you are not alone. God knows when you are frightened, and He wants to help you through it. He can give you the strength and courage to do the impossible. He can help you face any situation. He will help you meet new people and speak to them easily. For how else will you be able to tell them about Him?

God is always with you. Remember that when you face anything that frightens you. Just look to Him—He's standing right there beside you, just waiting to help you.

Whisper of Wisdom

*But Jesus immediately said to them:
"Take courage! It is I. Don't be afraid."*
MATTHEW 14:27 NIV

The Face in the Mirror

*Did you know. . .that being unhappy with who
you are—and how you look—hurts God's heart?*

If you were an actress, pretending to be someone you're not would be fun, wouldn't it? But in the real world, it's better to just be yourself. God made you. . .you! And He did it on purpose!

Think about it—the King of kings, your Daddy-God, decided even before you were born just what you would look like. He specially selected the color of your hair, your skin, your eyes—everything! He decided how tall or short you would be, how musical, how athletic. . .and dropped in some extra-special talents and abilities, just for fun! Your awesome Creator took great care in making all of these very important decisions.

When God looks at you, He loves what He sees! So the next time you look in the mirror and want to grumble, take the time to thank Him for making you. . .you!

Whisper of Wisdom

*"Before I shaped you in the womb, I knew all about you.
Before you saw the light of day, I had holy plans for you."*
JEREMIAH 1:5 MSG

Loving Lips

What's coming out of your lips?
The good. . .the bad. . .or the ugly?

What would someone else say about what comes out of your mouth? Would those around you say that you are always building people up or tearing people down? Do good things come out of your lips, or are you known for always speaking your mind whether it's good, bad, or ugly?

The Bible has a lot to say about what should come out of our mouths! Ephesians 4:29 tells us not to let anything bad come out of our mouths, but only what might build another person up. Proverbs 10:19; 11:12; and 17:28 tell us that it is often better to hold our tongues than to say something we may regret. So be careful what you allow to come out of your mouth! Remember that once something passes through your lips, you cannot take it back! Use your words to build people up, and let your lips be filled with praise for the Lord!

Whisper of Wisdom

May my lips overflow with praise,
for you teach me your decrees.
PSALM 119:171 NIV

Good Pain

Compliments are uplifting. Flattery is vain.
Constructive criticism only hurts for a time.

Everyone loves to hear a word of praise from time to time. Praise is good when it is honest and sincere. If your friend's new outfit really looks great on her, tell her. That compliment might really make her day.

If her new outfit doesn't do much for her, don't lie about it. Telling her she looks nice when she really doesn't is called flattery. It is unkind and deceitful.

Don't be rude. If she asks what you think of the outfit, you don't need to tell her it's ugly or that it makes her look fat. You can kindly mention how nice it is that she got a new outfit, and then remind her of how good she looks in another color or style. When done properly, constructive criticism only hurts momentarily.

Whisper of Wisdom

Faithful are the wounds of a friend;
but the kisses of an enemy are deceitful.

PROVERBS 27:6 KJV

I Can't See, but I Believe

What does your faith in Jesus mean to you?
It's the key to your eternal life as a child of God.

Lindsay's alarm went off at 6:57 a.m. She slapped the SNOOZE button, believing that the alarm would jolt her awake nine minutes later.

After she finally did get up, she rubbed the sleep out of her eyes as she squeezed a dollop of toothpaste onto her toothbrush. She turned on the faucet, trusting that the pipes in the wall would transport the water to her bathroom sink.

After booting up her laptop, she clicked PRINT and had faith her ink-jet printer would spit out the ten-page social studies report due that day at school.

On her way to school, she crossed the street on the crosswalk, having full confidence the cars driving down the street would obey the crossing guard's stop sign.

"Why do you believe in Jesus?" a friend asked Lindsay at lunch when she saw her reading her Bible. "What if He's just a nice story that people made up but He never really existed?"

"I believe in lots of things I can't see," Lindsay said. "That's what faith is—knowing something is true and not needing to have proof. His love for me is real, and so is the home in heaven He's preparing for me."

Whisper of Wisdom

Faith is the confidence that what we hope for will actually happen; it gives us assurance about things we cannot see.

HEBREWS 11:1 NLT

"All of My Friends Are Doing It!"

As a Christian, you should be set apart, living a life that would make Jesus proud. Not only should you do what is right, but you should also expose what is wrong.

Often it's easiest to give in to peer pressure by following the crowd in doing things that would disappoint Jesus and upset your parents. A better but more difficult choice is to just avoid those situations. But even in that choice, there is one more step to take—standing up for what's right.

Need an example? What if some kids you know were taunting a little girl who could use a good bath and is wearing raggedy clothes? Would you join in with the teasers or defend their target?

God wants you not only to refrain from doing wrong but to stand up for what's right. What is right is taking darkness and exposing it to the light. You aren't called to "get by" among your friends by just not doing wrong things. You're called to take a stand and teach others about their wrongdoings.

This is very difficult because it can cause problems with friends and peers. No one wants to be the outsider. But Jesus was the biggest outsider of all. He took a stand for you in the face of the greatest ridicule. Show Jesus how much you love Him by being willing to reject wrong and take a stand for right.

Whisper of Wisdom

Don't take part in doing those worthless things that are done in the dark. Instead, show how wrong they are.

EPHESIANS 5:11 CEV

The Quest

Think you can't? With God's help, you can!

Legends tell of heroes sent on spectacular quests—to slay the fire-breathing dragon, find the lost ring, or rescue the princess from a tower. All of these things seemed impossible. But with a little luck and some unexpected help, the hero managed to do it.

What's your impossible quest? Would you rather tackle the dragon than sing your solo? Are the answers to the upcoming math test as difficult to find as the missing ring? Does a lonely tower sound better than reading your book report in front of the class? Have courage! You have a powerful Helper on your side!

Prayer is the sword against the dragon, the finder of the missing ring, and the key to the tower. God has an unlimited supply of courage designed to defeat nervous jitters. He knows the answer to every math question. With Him at your side, you can do anything! As long as you have done your best by practicing, studying, and working hard, God is happy to help.

Step boldly up to the microphone. . .wield your pencil with confidence. . .read that report with your head held high. God is right there with you, helping you fulfill your quest.

Whisper of Wisdom

I can do all things through Christ which strengtheneth me.
PHILIPPIANS 4:13 KJV

At Your Service

Is serving a chore?
Hard work? Or a joy?

When you think of a leader, what comes to mind? Is it someone who tells people what to do? Someone who makes rules and demands that other people follow them?

While an effective leader *will* make rules and require that people follow instructions, leadership goes beyond that. A good leader serves others, too. Think of Jesus. He taught people what God commands, but He was a servant as well. He took a towel and bowl of water and washed His disciples' dirty feet (John 13:3-17). He did that, He said, to be an example of how they—and we—should treat others.

Is there a way you can be a servant today, to demonstrate the example that Jesus was to us? Maybe you could help an elderly person or someone who is sick. Ask your parents or someone at your church what you can do to help someone else. Showing love in this way will bring glory to Jesus.

Whisper of Wisdom

"Do you want to stand out? Then step down.
Be a servant. If you puff yourself up, you'll get
the wind knocked out of you. But if you're content
to simply be yourself, your life will count for plenty."
MATTHEW 23:11 MSG

It's Sooo Tempting!

*When someone you dislike gets into trouble,
what do you do? Do you secretly laugh behind her back?
Or do you say a prayer for her?*

Sally, a not-so-nice girl in your class, gets caught passing a note to her friend, and the teacher reads it out loud. Sally slumps in her chair, her face red with humiliation. Oh, it's so tempting. . . . You want to laugh out loud. Deep inside, you're rejoicing at her embarrassment. You think, *It's about time! Finally, she gets what she deserves! Now Miss Big Stuff isn't so big after all!*

But then you hear the still, small voice of Jesus. And He's disappointed in *your* behavior.

Jesus is sad when we find satisfaction in the hurts and embarrassments of others. And after all, you *do* know better.

As Christians, we're to love others—that means *all* people, including our enemies. And although it's a hard thing to do, that means reaching out and supporting them in Christian love rather than finding pleasure in their hardships. Say a prayer for your enemies today, and ask God to help you shine your light for Him.

Whisper of Wisdom

*Don't rejoice when your enemies fall;
don't be happy when they stumble.*

PROVERBS 24:17 NLT

The Princess Move

What do you do when two want to share the same space?
Is it time to stand your ground—or not?

When parents welcome their first baby, the child catches on that she has center stage, but she soon learns to share that stage when the next baby is born. God's family includes lots of other children, and that's why God asks each princess to graciously "move over" and make room for someone else.

When someone beats you to the shower in the morning and uses nearly all the hot water, God invites you to keep your cool. Rushing out the door, you notice a younger sibling struggling with a shoestring knot. God nudges you to set aside your plans for a second and stoop down to help. When a girl in your class shows up in the outfit you wanted to buy, although at first disappointed, you quickly begin to consider a few other outfits you liked that might look even better on you!

In edgy situations, God asks you to edge over—graciously. When you do, you won't step on someone else's toes. Don't worry—God may encourage another princess to move over and give you some space, too.

Whisper of Wisdom

Put up with each other, and forgive
anyone who does you wrong.

Colossians 3:13 cev

Worrywart!

I wonder if this will happen? I wonder if that will happen?
I hope everything turns out okay.

*H*ave you ever heard the expression "Don't be a worrywart"? If you're a worrier, you probably get upset over things before they even happen. You fear the worst.

So are you a worrywart? Let's find out.

Imagine you've got a big math test coming up. Math isn't your best subject. You study, but you're still worried you won't do well. The night before the test, you can hardly sleep. You toss and turn for hours, fretting over how you'll do on the test—what kind of grade you'll make, what your teacher will say, how your parents will react.

You start to imagine all sorts of things. "Will I pass math this year? Will I fail? Will I have to go to summer school?"

You can worry all night long, but it won't make things any better. In fact, it can only make things worse! God tells us in His Word that we aren't supposed to worry about tomorrow. So leave it up to God to handle the tough stuff. Do the best you can—then rest easy.

Whisper of Wisdom

"What I'm trying to do here is get you to relax, not be so preoccupied with getting so you can respond to God's giving. . . . Steep yourself in God-reality, God-initiative, God-provisions. You'll find all your everyday human concerns will be met."

LUKE 12:29, 31 MSG

Immediate Obedience

Parents aren't perfect. They make mistakes just like everyone else. But it makes Jesus happy when you immediately obey your parents, even when you think they're wrong.

A little girl was about to cross the street to get to the other side where her daddy was. As she stepped off the curb, her eyes on her daddy and her hands on her new bike, her dad yelled, "Step back, *now*!" Without even a glance to the left or right, the little girl, eyes still on her father, stepped back onto the curb. A car raced by—the car that was about to run her over.

Now, if she had taken a moment to question him or to look for a reason to disobey him, she would have been hit. It was her immediate obedience of her father's voice that saved her life. She was conditioned to believe that, even when she didn't understand it, her father was looking out for her best interests and had more understanding than she did.

We need to practice that kind of immediate obedience with our earthly parents and our heavenly Father, who work together for our greatest good.

Whisper of Wisdom

Be ye followers of me, even as I also am of Christ.

1 Corinthians 11:1 kjv

Spoiled Milk

Do your friends encourage you or bring you down?
God knows the importance of good influence.

Have you ever taken a drink out of the milk jug from the refrigerator only to find that it's spoiled? Rotten milk tastes worse than it smells, and the putrid aftertaste is terrible.

Nothing—not chocolate syrup or a powdered drink mix or cookies to dunk—can make the spoiled milk taste better. It's good for nothing and can only be dumped down the drain.

Our lives can become like spoiled milk when we spend time with friends who pressure us to do things we shouldn't. God knows that bad influences can bring down the most faithful and righteous person. That's why it's so important to choose our friends carefully. Although it's important to reach out to non-Christians, it's also important to have a core group of friends who share our beliefs and who can encourage us to make good decisions.

Are you a good influence on your friends? Ask God to show you how to be a better friend to the people around you. A little encouragement can go a long way.

Whisper of Wisdom

Do not be misled: "Bad company corrupts good character."
1 CORINTHIANS 15:33 NIV

Be Like Jesus

Be like Jesus by obeying His commands.

A lot of today's movies and TV shows portray people breaking the Ten Commandments and then some. With such examples of bad behavior constantly in front of us, it's easy to forget what Jesus wants us to do.

God originally gave us all the Ten Commandments or the "thou shalt nots" in Exodus 20. You know, "Thou shalt not kill. . .commit adultery. . .steal. . .bear false witness [lie]. . .covet. . ." And before all those is the verse saying you *shall* "honour thy father and thy mother" (KJV). Later, when Jesus came along, He echoed His Father's Ten Commandments and then wrapped them all up in two statements that cover them all: "Love the Lord your God," and "Love your neighbor as yourself" (Matthew 22:37-39 NIV).

So no matter what you see in TV shows and movies and on the six o'clock news, remember what Jesus wants *you* to do. Don't hurt anyone, don't be unfaithful, steal, lie, envy others, and so forth. Treat your parents with respect and honor, and treat others just as you would want them to treat you.

To sum it all up, don't be like the world. Be like Jesus by loving everyone and, even more important, loving God with all your heart, soul, strength, and mind. When you do, you'll make the world a better place for yourself and everyone around you!

Whisper of Wisdom

Jesus [said], "Do not murder, do not commit adultery, do not steal, do not give false testimony, honor your father and mother," and "love your neighbor as yourself."

MATTHEW 19:18-19 NIV

A Wise Use of Time

It always seems there's a lot to do with little time to do it.
But with a little planning, you can achieve the wise use of time.

Are you the kind of student who dives right into her homework when she gets home from school? Are you the kind of girl who gets right to the task when it's time to clean her room, resisting the urge to read all of those notes from a friend? It's easy to get distracted and find tons of "little things" to do rather than doing the greater task at hand.

We each have twenty-four hours in our day, although the way we spend that time may differ greatly. Of course, we need to sleep and eat, and usually we do both of those without much thought or planning.

But what about spending time with God? That should also be part of our daily routine. And God wants you to do your best in your work—school and chores.

Why not pray and ask God for His help in spending your time wisely? That would be a great use of time!

Whisper of Wisdom

Those who are wise will find a time
and a way to do what is right.

ECCLESIASTES 8:5 NLT

The Greatest Gift

The most valuable present is appreciation.

What are you getting Mom for her birthday?" eleven-year-old Kimberly asked her little brother on their way to the school bus stop.

"I think I'll give her my Blasto-8000," Kevin said.

"You're going to give her a used squirt gun?" Kimberly's eyes grew wide with disbelief. "You're supposed to give someone a gift *they'll* like, not one *you'd* like."

"But I don't have any money," Kevin said, his thin shoulders slumping. "I thought maybe if I gave her something really special to me, she'd know that she's really special, too."

Kimberly thought about his words. "You know, Kev, you might have something there. I know the Bible says children are a gift to their parents, but I think sometimes we forget to let our parents know we think they're a gift to us, too."

Kevin grinned. "So what are you going to give her—your *High School Musical* poster?"

"Nooo." Kimberly smiled back, ruffling his hair. "But I just might wrap up my favorite stuffed animal with a note telling her that just like Bear-Bear always had a hug for me when I needed one, I appreciate the way she's always been there when I needed her."

Whisper of Wisdom

Children are a gift from the Lord;
they are a reward from him.

Psalm 127:3 NLT

Greater Than Rubies

You are priceless to God. You are precious to others.
You are of greater value than rare jewels.

Alexis slowly turned the pages of her mother's scrapbook. As she enjoyed each memory, she discovered a younger version of herself. She found herself dressed in the fancy clothes of a fine lady. Her neck and wrists were adorned with lovely jewelry. She vaguely remembered the day her mother had allowed her to play with her great-grandmother's pretty things.

"She was a wonderful lady, Lexi," her mother had said. "She was beautiful and graceful, but she was so much more than that. She had lovely things, but they looked pale next to her. She had godly virtues. She was gentle and kind. She loved her family and worked hard to give them a good life. She was helpful to others, and everyone loved her. You're adorable in her fine things, Lexi. I just pray that you will become the virtuous woman that she was."

Alexis barely remembered her great-grandmother, and she didn't fully understand what virtue was all about, but she was determined to do her best to be like this woman who was so much like Christ.

Whisper of Wisdom

Who can find a virtuous woman?
For her price is far above rubies.
PROVERBS 31:10 KJV

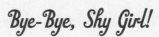

Bye-Bye, Shy Girl!

Feeling shy? Not as outgoing as you'd like to be?
With God's help, you can be confident to let your personality shine!

It's normal to be nervous anytime you reveal something genuine and personal about yourself to others. Whether you're singing a solo in front of a group of friends from school or church, sharing a story you wrote in front of the class, or simply sharing your faith with one of your friends, any of these things can be scary if you try to do it in your own strength.

Remember that the Spirit of God can help you overcome your nervousness. If God has given you a song to sing, a story to tell, or a message to share with a certain friend, pray for His strength and His power to work through you and then go for it! Give it all you've got. Be bold and strong, for God is with you!

Whisper of Wisdom

For the Spirit God gave us does not make us timid,
but gives us power, love and self-discipline.
2 Timothy 1:7 tniv

Pleasing Our Father

This is My daughter. . .whom I love.

Imagine a little princess in the throne room, sitting at her Father's feet while He rules the kingdom. As she just sits in His presence, looking up at Him with stars in her eyes, He knows how much she loves Him. It brings such joy to His heart when she wants to spend time with Him.

Like your earthly parents, God enjoys everything about you. He loved watching when you began to walk, and He celebrated when you learned to play patty-cake. He has been there for every victory, cheering you on. Through your ups and your downs, He's been watching—and smiling.

God is especially pleased when you obey your parents and the other adults in your life. That really makes Him happy! He loves it when you do the right thing, especially without being asked (like doing your chores without having to be reminded). Why? Because it shows Him that you are learning. You're growing.

Best of all, God is thrilled when you love Him with your whole heart. This makes Him happiest of all.

Whisper of Wisdom

For [Jesus] received honor and glory from God the Father when the voice came to him from the Majestic Glory, saying, "This is my Son, whom I love; with him I am well pleased."

2 PETER 1:17 NIV

The Gift

Salvation cannot be earned;
it is freely offered as a gift for you to simply receive.

There is a difference between receiving a birthday gift and earning something by doing chores or by earning money in some way. The birthday gift is freely given with no desire for repayment or anything more than appreciation. But when you have to earn something yourself, it requires effort and struggle, and sometimes even then it's not possible to get what you were after.

Salvation is like that birthday gift. It's offered to you freely. In no way is it something you can earn or deserve. It is completely given to you by God. Jesus bought the gift with His own life, and He offers it to you with no repayment required. All you need to do is receive the gift and accept your salvation. This gift of God includes the forgiveness of your sins and the right for you to spend eternity with Jesus in heaven.

Receive God's gracious gift today by praying and asking Him to come into your life and receiving His salvation.

Whisper of Wisdom

For it is by grace you have been saved, through faith—
and this not from yourselves, it is the gift of God.

EPHESIANS 2:8 NIV

The Princess Heart

*A good princess exercise is to choose
what will fit best in the space you have.*

What things go in your purse when you head out to school? Lunch money, a pen or pencil, your hairbrush? In the same way you figure out what you can make room for in your purse, you'll also decide what you will make room for in your life. You'll make space for what's important to you. It might be sports, entertainment, grades, books, or clothes. Like a man named Paul, you might want to top your list with "people."

No matter where this traveling missionary went, Paul figured out a way to find time and space for people. Mostly, Paul shared the good news of Jesus Christ with people he met, but he also showed he cared about them by sticking around and getting to know them.

So whatever else you enjoy, why not make room for people around you? They'll appreciate the time and space you share with them. Hey, for fun, check out the sixteenth chapter of Romans to see how Paul crowded people into his life, not out of it.

Whisper of Wisdom

*We loved you so much that we were delighted to share with
you not only the gospel of God but our lives as well.*

1 THESSALONIANS 2:8 NIV

Responsibility

God wants you to respect and follow your church leaders, because they are responsible to Him for you.

God made mama lions to take care of their cubs, to watch over them and teach them, so that someday the cubs can take care of themselves. Because, let's face it, it's a jungle out there.

In the same way, God gave you parents to take care of you and teach you to stand on your own two feet. And to help you even more, God has also placed leaders in your church, people who can guide you and train you up in the way He wants you to grow. Those leaders—your pastor, youth leader, Sunday school teacher, children's church teacher, and so on—are accountable to God for you.

You can help God by submitting to your church leaders' authority so that their work will be a joy. They have a big responsibility. So make God, yourself, and your leaders happy by listening to them and following their guidance. Because before you know it, you'll be on your own and perhaps leading children yourself! How cool and joyful that will be!

Whisper of Wisdom

Obey your leaders and submit to their authority.
They keep watch over you as men who must give an
account. Obey them so that their work will be a joy,
not a burden, for that would be of no advantage to you.

HEBREWS 13:17 NIV

Top-Secret Beauty Tip

What's the secret to looking your best?
Trendy clothes. . .adorable shoes. . .gorgeous hair? Guess again!

*T*here's just something about being a girl. You love to dress up! Pretty clothes with shoes to match. . .your hair up in curls. . .sparkly barrettes. . .a cute purse. . .the list goes on and on. And why shouldn't you look your best? You are, after all, a daughter of the King!

But fancy clothes and all of the matching accessories aren't necessary to make you truly beautiful. In fact, the most important thing you can wear can't be bought at a store. It was given to you by God Himself. Can you guess what it is? Your *smile*!

Smiling is a reflection of the beauty *inside* you. It's hard to frown when you're bubbling over with joy. And there's nothing more beautiful than the expression of that joy—your very own smile.

So don't worry about whether or not your teeth are straight. *Smile!* Use your God-given beauty accessory to welcome the new girl, comfort a gloomy friend, and share your happiness—all without saying a single word. You won't have to. Your smile says it all!

Whisper of Wisdom

A glad heart makes a happy face.
PROVERBS 15:13 NLT

Nothing to Fear

The angel at the tomb said there is nothing to fear.
Hold on to that same promise today.

Imagine what it was like for Mary and Mary Magdalene to walk to Jesus' tomb early Easter morning.

They were sad that Jesus had died two days before. Probably teary, the two women may have talked about their memories of the Messiah during His life. It was a morning walk of mourning.

But their mourning changed in an instant as they came across a man dressed in white. Their hearts probably skipped a few beats when they saw the stone rolled away and the body of Jesus nowhere to be found.

The words of the angel probably came in the split second before the women were convinced they were going completely nuts: "There is nothing to fear here. . . . He was raised, just as he said."

Even today Christians have nothing to fear. Because of Jesus' resurrection, we have confidence that the plan God crafted for us—eternity with Him—is a gift we can count on. Jesus defeated Satan on the day the angel told the world, "There is nothing to fear here."

Whisper of Wisdom

"There is nothing to fear here. I know you're looking
for Jesus, the One they nailed to the cross.
He is not here. He was raised, just as he said.
Come and look at the place where he was placed."

MATTHEW 28:5-6 MSG

Never Lonely

On days when you feel like you're all alone, remember that you have a friend who will be there for you—always. He wouldn't desert you for anything—not even the best party of the year.

*A*ll my friends are at Olivia's birthday party—the birthday party I wasn't invited to. I want to lock myself in my room for the entire weekend and cry, thought Kiley. *It's not fair. I can't believe my best friends in the whole world would ditch me like this!*

We all have lonely moments from time to time—moments when we feel like no one cares, no one wants to listen to our problems, no one wants to spend time with us. . . And in those moments we can choose to be sad and miserable, or we can choose to find comfort in the One who will never leave us lonely.

Our heavenly Father promises that He'll always be here for us, even when our friends and family let us down. When there's no one for us to turn to, we can always talk to God. He'll listen; He'll comfort; He'll encourage. He's always there—24/7. And He's waiting to hear from you now!

Whisper of Wisdom

"I am with you always, even to the end of the world."
MATTHEW 28:20 NLV

Hello! Can You Hear Me?

Remember, prayer is just talking to God.
You can call on Him anytime, anywhere. He's listening.

We spend a lot of our time trying to contact people—by telephone and computer, for the most part. How many times have you tried to reach a friend, only to find the line was busy, or you had to leave a message on her voice mail, or you found that she wasn't online and had to wait for a reply e-mail? Waiting can be frustrating, especially when you need to talk with someone immediately.

The God who made you is always ready to listen whenever you call on Him, and no request is too small to take to Him. He will never send you to voice mail or put you on hold.

Talk to Him when you have a problem, when you need forgiveness, or when you want to praise or thank Him. Just talk with Him—He's waiting to hear from you!

Whisper of Wisdom

Know that the LORD has set apart the godly for himself;
the LORD will hear when I call to him.

PSALM 4:3 NIV

Off the Slide, Princess!

Before climbing a slide, do you look to see how steep it is?
Good idea, too, to check where you'll end up!

If you sit at the top of a waterslide, the next step is "flying" downhill into deep water. Great fun for a good swimmer, but hang on before you venture down a "money slide." The slippery slope begins when you allow money to get into your heart instead of keeping it in your billfold or bank account where it belongs.

So how can God's princess keep from falling in love with money? Choose, instead, to fill your heart with the riches of God's Word. Read it, memorize it, and obey it. How about using today's Bible verse as a good starting point? As your King, God uses His words to help you keep your heart free of the love of money.

Money can buy lots of stuff, but it can't buy the things you need the most, like favor with God, family, or friendships. At all costs, keep from letting the love of money pull you down that slippery slope.

Whisper of Wisdom

The love of money causes all kinds of trouble.
1 TIMOTHY 6:10 CEV

Good Mouth, Bad Mouth

To your face. . .behind your back. . .
you can trust me to speak good things about you!

Imagine this: You're hanging out with your best friend, Jessica, when a new girl named Becca walks by. Jessica makes a comment about Becca's hair. . .or maybe her clothes. You know you shouldn't bad-mouth someone, but what's the harm in talking about her behind her back? After all, she'll never find out. . .right?

Truth is, the Bible teaches that we are to treat people with kindness—to their faces and behind their backs. We have to watch the words that come out of our mouth. God tells us in the Bible that we are to treat others the way we want to be treated. (This is called the "Golden Rule.")

So how do you want to be treated? Better watch out! If you dish it out (gossiping, bad-mouthing, or cutting people down), you're telling God that that's the way you want to be treated. Ouch! When you think about it like that, it sure doesn't sound like much fun, does it?

Whisper of Wisdom

Don't bad-mouth each other, friends.
It's God's Word, his Message, his Royal Rule,
that takes a beating in that kind of talk.
JAMES 4:11 MSG

What Is Your Purpose?

You're learning to become a responsible young woman.
So what is your purpose?

King Solomon had it all. He was famous. He was powerful. Hey, he was the richest, wisest man on earth. He was also dissatisfied with his life, and he spent a lot of time trying to figure out what his purpose was.

You see, Solomon had once walked closely with God. God had been his closest friend, but Solomon became distracted. He looked at all the pleasures that the world had to offer, and he thought he had to try them. He spent lots of time and money to obtain many things, but he soon realized that none of this would bring him any happiness.

As Solomon grew older, he began to ponder why all of these things he'd worked so hard for didn't bring him any lasting pleasure. Do you know what he discovered? It was a truth he'd known all along. God had to be first in his life.

The same goes for you. If "things" are your main concern, you'll never be fully satisfied. If God is first, you'll always know true joy.

Whisper of Wisdom

Let us hear the conclusion of the whole matter: Fear God, and
keep his commandments: for this is the whole duty of man.
ECCLESIASTES 12:13 KJV

Worldly Poison

Be very careful what you allow to pass before your eyes. What you watch, what you allow in your life, will begin to change you.

Have you ever been stung by a bee? It hurts a lot! But did you know that the bee only deposits a tiny, tiny bit of poison into you? That little bit of poison is what hurts so bad! Eventually your wound begins to swell and becomes inflamed. It will even be sore for days.

The poison in a bee's stinger is like the influence of the world on a Christian. Just a little bit of bad language or a few wrong pictures can have a bad effect on a person's thoughts. When we allow ourselves to be exposed to a little bit of the world's poison, even though we don't plan to let it take hold, we begin to become less sensitive to those behaviors. Slowly, some of them will creep into our lives while we are unaware. Satan likes to "sting" you by filling your thoughts with worldly poison. Don't let him! Ask Jesus to help you keep your mind and thoughts pure and unaffected by the world.

Whisper of Wisdom

I will refuse to look at anything vile and vulgar.

PSALM 101:3 NLT

In God's Will

Our heavenly Father wants to be the God of our nation.
Put God first in your life, and others will follow.

Most polls show that the majority of Americans believe in God's existence. The truth is that God wants to be more than a faraway belief to these millions of people.

God wants every person in the United States (and the world!) to have a relationship with Him, to believe in His Son, Jesus, and to accept His gift of grace and eternal life.

The fact is that the United States has been blessed by God since its beginning more than two hundred years ago, and God wants to continue blessing our country until Jesus returns. We've had our rough patches and setbacks, but our blessings are too great to count: health, safety, prosperity, growth.

It's up to us to deepen our relationship with God. And then we must show others—friends, neighbors, family—the plan God has for them. That's when America will be truly blessed.

Whisper of Wisdom

Blessed is the country with GOD for God;
blessed are the people he's put in his will.

PSALM 33:12 MSG

Banished to the Tower

Even a princess gets in trouble sometimes.
It's all part of being God's child.

*Y*ou know what it's like. That "uh-oh" sensation that comes right after you've done something wrong. That terrible guilty feeling that overshadows your heart. You want to stop thinking about it, but you can't! You're utterly miserable and don't know what to do.

While it may feel like God has banished you to a gloomy tower, He's really trying to teach you a lesson. It's called *chastisement*, and it's God's way of keeping you from making the same bad decision again.

Chastisement hurts, and for good reason. Your heavenly Father loves you too much to let you slide when it comes to spiritual danger. When you make poor choices, His Spirit is right there to shake a disapproving finger. The worse you feel about your actions, the less likely you are to repeat them.

When you feel the chastising hand of God, don't run away from Him. Run *to* your loving Father in prayer. Thank Him for His faithful warning and show Him that you've learned your lesson by doing the right thing next time.

Whisper of Wisdom

As you endure this divine discipline, remember
that God is treating you as his own children.
HEBREWS 12:7 NLT

Everywhere Praise!

*Praise God wherever you go—at home, at school, at practice,
at church, while doing homework, with your friends.
He is worthy of all your praise—everywhere and anytime!*

God wants our worship more than just at church on Sunday morning. He's worthy of our praise more than just at weekly youth group and during our daily quiet time. He wants our prayer more often than before meals and at bedtime. He deserves our praise twenty-four hours a day, seven days every week.

The psalm writer knew the importance of praising God—church, home, work, school, inside, outside. Anywhere is the perfect place to praise!

With instruments, voices, art, athletics, sacrifice, and actions: Everything we do can glorify God!

What can you do today to spend more time praising God? Worship Him by telling a friend about something exciting He's doing in your life. Glorify His name by sharing with someone in need. Praise Him by showing love to someone who is unlovable. Praise Him, and you'll reap the benefits, too.

Whisper of Wisdom

*Praise God in his holy house of worship, praise him
under the open skies. . . . Praise with a blast on
the trumpet, praise by strumming soft strings. . . .
Let every living, breathing creature praise God!*

PSALM 150:1, 3, 6 MSG

Created in His Image

Do you know that you look like God? It's true! You do!

Have you ever wondered what God looks like? It's fun to imagine, isn't it? We won't know for sure until we get to heaven, but one thing is clear—you are created in His image.

So does that mean God has blond hair and freckles? Does it mean He wears tennis shoes? Does He like to go shopping and hang out with His friends after school?

Not exactly. To be created in the "image" of God means you look like Him on the inside. When you smile, it's His smile that's coming through. When you're sweet to others, it's His sweetness they see. When you stop to give someone a helping hand, it's like His hand is reaching out to them.

Every princess is created in the image of her Daddy-God. When people look at you, they see a shining reflection of Him. So the next time someone says, "Hey, you look like your dad!" just smile. They're right, you know.

Whisper of Wisdom

God created man in his own image,
in the image of God created he him;
male and female created he them.

GENESIS 1:27 KJV

God Is Great, God Is Good

God wants to give us joy!

The first day of fifth grade was scary for Jessie. Her family had moved into town only a week before, and she hadn't met any new friends yet—except the girl she sat next to in Sunday school yesterday. Lorna smiled but didn't say much.

Jessie had always been shy and hadn't had many friends in the town she'd moved from. Only Buffy, who had been her best friend since second grade. They'd shared everything—clothes, giggles, whispers into the night. And now Buffy was two hundred miles away.

"Lord," Jessie whispered as she stared at the huge double doors that led into the school, "please send me a friend. Just one, and I'll be happy."

A shrill bell rang, and kids flew through the double doors like bees into a hive. Jessie found her way to her classroom and chose a desk near the door. She began sorting the items in her pencil box when a voice softly called her name.

"Jessie?" Lorna took the seat beside her with a big smile. "I'm so glad to see you. I'm new here, too. I prayed for a friend, and just look what God did!"

Whisper of Wisdom

The Lord has done great things for us,
and we are filled with joy.

Psalm 126:3 niv

Someone's Watching

Know what? You've got an audience!
It's true—someone's always watching.

As a Christian girl today, you will have lots of people watching every move you make as you grow up. People are watching to see if you are really living out what you believe. Why? Because everyone wants to know if what you believe makes a difference in your life!

If you are truly living out your faith every day and others can see a difference in you, you just might find some of your observers checking out this "Christian thing" for themselves. Does this worry you a little? Make sure you are living a life that is pleasing to the Lord. Get rid of anything that might be hindering your relationship with Him, and ask Him to help you live out your faith each day.

Whisper of Wisdom

Therefore, since we are surrounded by such a great
cloud of witnesses, let us throw off everything that
hinders and the sin that so easily entangles, and let
us run with perseverance the race marked out for us.

HEBREWS 12:1 NIV

Have a Little Faith

*Believe in the Lord and know
that He is with you always.*

When it's hard to tell your friends you won't do something because you know it's wrong, and you feel all alone, remember that God is always there to help you stand up for what's right. Don't be afraid. He will give you the courage to say no and then to stand your ground.

Do you know how many times the Bible tells us not to be afraid? Three hundred and sixty-five. That means for every day of the year, there is a verse telling you that you need not fear. No matter what the situation, Jesus will never leave you or forsake you. That's a powerful Friend to have by your side every minute of every day and night! What an amazing God we have.

So never fear, princess. Your Father, your King, your Savior is only a prayer away to help you withstand pressure—whether it's from fear or peers! Just have a little faith and you'll be fine!

Whisper of Wisdom

"Have faith in God," Jesus answered.

MARK 11:22 NIV

The Best of Both Worlds

Can you have everything you want out of life?
Only if everything you want is to put God first as Lord.

Can you live like a spoiled pop star and still serve God? Can you go to church on Sunday and forget about God's rules Monday through Saturday? No way.

Say you are friends with Erica, but you also want to hang out with the popular girls who say mean things to Erica. You can't have both for long. Soon your friendship with those girls will hurt Erica's feelings, and she won't trust you as her friend again.

A mature young woman will pick the right way to behave and stick to it.

Old-timers would say that "the grass isn't always greener on the other side of the fence." Though it may look appealing and fun on the other side, choosing to go against how God teaches us to live and to treat others will only lead us to pain. Having a bit of fun is nothing if you don't have God's blessing. So make sure you're always in God's yard. He has the greenest grass!

Whisper of Wisdom

"No servant can serve two masters. Either he will hate the one and love the other, or he will be devoted to the one and despise the other."

LUKE 16:13 NIV

Princess Proverb

*A wise princess learns from wise
sayings like "Haste makes waste."*

Will your parents detect the pile of dirty laundry stuffed under your bed or the overflowing wastebasket in the corner? If *their* idea of cleaning demands too much of your time, will they approve of your shortcut methods? Hey, ask Cain about shortcuts.

When Adam and Eve's sons Cain and Abel grew up, each presented an offering to God. Abel wanted to please God and gladly sacrificed some of the best of his flock, but Cain apparently wasn't into that kind of detail. So he decided on a "better" plan that required little effort or cost on his part. If he had to give, why not do it the easy way? With luck on his side, maybe God wouldn't notice.

Well, God saw a huge difference between Abel's *want to* offering and Cain's *have to* offering. Instead of doing the least, why not do your best? A wise princess pays attention to details, and so does her King.

Whisper of Wisdom

*The LORD had regard for Abel and his offering, but He did
not have regard for Cain and his offering. Cain was furious.*

GENESIS 4:4-5 HCSB

Life Overload

So many activities demand your time.
Is your schedule under control?

What do you have to do today? Go to a music lesson? Attend sports practice? So many events and activities can make you feel as if you're pulled in a dozen different directions. While there isn't anything wrong with wanting to develop talents and abilities, sometimes the hectic pace can bring a lot of stress.

If you're feeling a little burned out, take a few minutes to think about what consumes your time. Perhaps you feel like your schedule is a little too full. Ask your parents to discuss some options with you. It could be that you need to come up with a written schedule. Or maybe you'll find that you need to take a break from one of your activities.

Even on your busiest of days, don't forget to take some time out to meet with God. Read His Word and talk with Him. He gave you life, and He wants to be the Lord of it.

Whisper of Wisdom

"There will be a time for every activity,
a time for every deed."

ECCLESIASTES 3:17 NIV

Safe in God's Arms

You are one of God's precious lambs.
You have no need to fear; your Shepherd is always with you.

Isn't it wonderful to know that you are safe within the arms of your loving Shepherd? He cares for you as if you were the only lamb He had. Sometimes you might feel helpless, frightened, or all alone. If you let Him, those are the times that Jesus will draw you the closest and shelter you within His loving arms.

At other times you might feel confused. Remember: You can turn to God. He wants very much to lead you, and He knows the best way.

Then there will be days when there's nothing in particular on your mind. Those are the days you walk along with Jesus because you love Him, and you know how very much He loves you.

Never forget: You are God's precious lamb. He cares for you.

Whisper of Wisdom

He shall feed his flock like a shepherd: he shall gather
the lambs with his arm, and carry them in his bosom.

Isaiah 40:11 KJV

Scary Movie

Sometimes the things you're allowed to do aren't really the best things to do.

Brandy couldn't wait to turn thirteen. Since she was one of the youngest kids in her class, it seemed like she'd waited *forever* to be old enough to watch PG-13 movies with her friends.

Her first thirteen-year-old Friday night came with plans to go see the newest and best scary movie in the theater—complete with enough edge-of-your-seat suspense to scare the bravest among them.

Popcorn, Skittles, and Coke in hand, Brandy sat with friends, her heart pounding as she watched images of terror-filled faces as the victims ran through dark hallways. It was so scary that Brandy couldn't keep her eyes open. Even the music and sounds from the movie made her jump in her seat.

Later in her own bed, images from the movie kept Brandy from falling asleep. So she decided to pray.

God, now I know that movie wasn't something You wanted me to see. Please forgive me for being so excited to be allowed to see scary movies that I didn't stop to think if they are good for me. I want to do the things that will make You happy—and not freak me out. Now, Lord, please give me the peace to sleep. And thanks for listening. Amen.

Whisper of Wisdom

I pray that your love will keep on growing and that you will fully know and understand how to make the right choices. Then you will still be pure and innocent when Christ returns. And until that day, Jesus Christ will keep you busy doing good deeds that bring glory and praise to God.

Philippians 1:9–11 CEV

Dinnertime!

Are you hungry? Starving?
Well, dig in!

What if you found out you couldn't eat all day? Not one bite of food. What would you do? Would you make it? What if you couldn't eat for two days. . .or three? Then what? Chances are, you would be mighty weak! You'd probably also be cranky. (Some people start to grumble after missing just one meal!) Before long, your hunger would take over and you wouldn't be able to think about anything—except food!

Did you know that the Bible (the Word of God) is like food to our spirits? Seriously. If you go without reading it for a while, you get weak. And if you go without reading it for a very long time, your strength is completely zapped. So don't let your Bible sit there on the bedside table, gathering dust. Dig in, princess! A daughter of the King knows her Father's words. She memorizes them and quotes them when she needs a reminder that He's close by.

Feeling hungry? Reach for your Bible. Talk about a balanced diet!

Whisper of Wisdom

*For the word of God is alive and powerful. It is sharper
than the sharpest two-edged sword, cutting between
soul and spirit, between joint and marrow.
It exposes our innermost thoughts and desires.*

Hebrews 4:12 NLT

The Best Gift

A box of chocolates for Mom? Golf balls for Dad?
What's the best thing you can give your parents?

You want your mother and father to be proud of you. You want to be the model daughter. How do you do that? By playing the lead role in the school play? By wowing the audience at your piano recital? Getting straight A's on your report card? Acing the big test? Earning Student of the Year?

Well, chances are, your parents are already proud of you. You don't have to go out of your way to knock their socks off. In fact, there's only one thing that your parents expect from you. What is it?

Obedience.

Nothing thrills your parents more than when you obey. Agreeing to follow their rules without arguing and complaining is worth more than any gift you could give them. And not only does it make *them* happy; it pleases your heavenly Father as well.

Whether or not you agree with their rules, whether or not you understand their wishes. . .obey. Why? Because it's the *right* thing to do. And nothing will make your parents—both earthly and heavenly—happier.

Whisper of Wisdom

Children, obey your parents in the Lord:
for this is right.
EPHESIANS 6:1 KJV

What If?

Don't allow yourself to be held back by doubts. Ask God to take away your "what-ifs" and replace them with an even stronger faith in Him and His promises.

Some days you may find yourself asking a lot of what-if questions. *What if I don't make the team? What if I forget my lines for the school play? What if I embarrass myself in front of the entire school at the talent show?*

Everyone struggles with the fear of failure at one time or another. But God doesn't want us to give up on something before we even get started. That's why He encourages us to talk to Him about our worries and then leave the details to Him. He'll support you in whatever you seek to accomplish.

Today ask God to erase those nerve-racking what-ifs from your mind, and believe that He will provide just the right amount of courage and strength that you need. With God on your side, you'll be amazed at what you can do. That's a promise!

Whisper of Wisdom

*"Peace I leave with you; my peace I give you.
I do not give to you as the world gives. Do not let
your hearts be troubled and do not be afraid."*

JOHN 14:27 NIV

Do unto Others

Knowing how to interact with others comes down to a very simple principle: Only do to others what you would want them to do to you.

Many opportunities in life seem to require you to step on the toes of someone else so that you can get ahead. Getting a job, going after a leadership position in school, getting out of trouble of some kind—those are all situations in which it may be tempting to treat someone badly to get what you want.

It's not okay to do that, though. No achievement is worth it if it involves hurting someone else. And when you're faced with trouble, it's never acceptable to put all of the blame on someone else so that you can avoid the heat.

God wants you to treat other people just as you hope to be treated by them. That's a perfect measuring tool for behavior toward others. If you are in doubt about what is right or wrong, just ask yourself how you would feel if someone did it to you. What is right will become immediately clear.

Whisper of Wisdom

Treat others just as you want to be treated.
LUKE 6:31 CEV

You Are Well Created

*On day six God made people. His creation was very good.
You, His child, were created just right.*

God made countless wonderful things during those first few days of creation, and at the end of each day, He looked back over all He had made and saw that it was good.

On the sixth day God had something special planned. He would make Adam and Eve—the very first people. Each detail was planned completely, and after He breathed life into them, He saw that His creation was *very* good. It was complete.

When God made you, His creation was again very good. He designed you in a special way. You are the only one of you there will ever be, and only you can do the job God has prepared for you. When you are tempted to look down on yourself, remember: God always gets it right!

Whisper of Wisdom

*God saw every thing that he had made, and,
behold, it was very good. And the evening
and the morning were the sixth day.*

GENESIS 1:31 KJV

My First Love

Love. . .as easy as 1, 2, 3!

Did you ever think about what it's going to be like to fall in love for the very first time? Well, guess what—God is your first love, and He has the best plan for how you can love others, too!

1. Love God more than anything. *Whoa! Seriously? More than my parents? My friends? My clothes? My stuff?* Yep. Start by putting your love for your heavenly Father above every other thing. Love Him with all of your heart, soul, mind, and strength. That's a lot of love!

2. Love yourself. *It's okay to love myself?* Sure! If you don't love yourself, it's pretty hard to love others. You just have to remember not to put yourself first—above God. It's not all about you, after all. It's all about Him.

3. Love others as you love yourself. *You mean everyone?* Yep. Everyone! And put their needs above your own, even when it's hard. Remember that God loves them just as much as He loves you.

Go forth and love, princess!

Whisper of Wisdom

"'Love the Lord your God with all your heart and with all your soul and with all your mind and with all your strength.' The second is this: 'Love your neighbor as yourself.' There is no commandment greater than these."

MARK 12:30-31 NIV

Home, Sweet Home

Where do you call home?
If you're a child of God, your home is in heaven.

When people asked Emma where she was from, she never knew how to answer. She was born in Indiana, but her family moved to Georgia when she was two. She started kindergarten in Arizona and had gone to four schools in three different states since then. Now as a fifth-grader in Virginia, she just wanted to live somewhere long enough that she could feel like herself and make a few close friends.

As Emma grew stronger in her faith and closer in her relationship with Jesus, she began to find scriptures that helped her figure out where her true home really is. Heaven, she read, is where God is preparing a place where she will truly be home.

"Dear Jesus," Emma wrote in her prayer journal. *"Sometimes I feel like I don't have a real home, that I don't truly 'belong' anywhere. You know what that feels like. But You have prepared the way for me and all of Your followers to live at home in heaven forever with You. Thank You for making a room in Your home just for me."*

Whisper of Wisdom

We are citizens of heaven, where the Lord Jesus Christ lives. And we are eagerly waiting for him to return as our Savior.

PHILIPPIANS 3:20 NLT

The Praying Stance

Forgive and then let it go.

Sometimes when we start to pray, we find we have bad feelings about someone. When this happens, we need to think about it, because to be forgiven by God, we need to forgive others. Whether or not others know they've harmed us, whether or not the hurt was intentional, we need to bring our anger and resentment before God and forgive them.

So if you are carrying a grudge against someone because you think he treated you badly, forgive him and then let it go. If you are angry at a friend because she didn't do what you wanted her to or even because she's mad at you, forgive her and then let it go. If you resent someone because she got a better grade than you did or the teacher was nicer to her today, forgive her and let it go. If you don't like someone because she doesn't like you, ask God to forgive you and to help you love her anyway, and then let it go.

If you want God to forgive you, you need to forgive others. So when you pray, forgive and then let it go. You'll feel better about things, and so will God!

Whisper of Wisdom

"When you stand praying, if you hold anything against anyone, forgive him, so that your Father in heaven may forgive you your sins."

MARK 11:25 NIV

Double Dipping

*Surely God doesn't care about table manners.
Or does He? You may be surprised at the answer!*

*O*nce you dip a chip into the salsa and take a bite, no more dipping! You may get by with double dipping at home, but not at the grocery store with Saturday morning samples. That's a rule you'd do well to obey. Do you know God made a rule about double dipping?

The Israelites learned a lesson about double dipping. God fed them with manna from heaven, but He commanded them to pick up what they needed for the day. They were to throw away what was left. God promised *fresh* manna the next day, but some ignored this rule and boxed up their leftovers. The next morning they found bugs in their breakfast! God was serious about no double dipping the second day.

When God provides what you need on Monday, do you believe God will come through on Tuesday, too? God says, "Trust Me, princess!"

Whisper of Wisdom

*Moses said to them, "No one is
to keep any of it until morning."
However, some of them paid no attention.*
EXODUS 16:19–20 NIV

Pray Anyway

Perhaps it isn't popular. There are places it's not even allowed.
But no one can really stop you from praying.

Think about Daniel for just a minute. He is a man with a lot of great stories to tell. It all started when he was a boy—maybe not a lot older than you. The powerful Babylonians captured Jerusalem, and Daniel was taken captive, but he certainly wasn't treated poorly. The king could tell Daniel was wise, so Daniel received an excellent education and royal treatment.

From the start, though, Daniel determined to stay true to God, and he remained faithful throughout his life. He knew that he would face the lions if he bowed to any but proud King Darius. But even in the face of that threat, Daniel openly prayed to God.

When you face taunting or rules saying you can't pray, be like Daniel and pray anyway. Stand true to God. Prayer is a gift from Him. Use it daily—no matter what.

Whisper of Wisdom

Now when Daniel knew that the writing was signed,
he went into his house; and his windows being open. . .
he kneeled upon his knees three times a day, and prayed,
and gave thanks before his God, as he did aforetime.

DANIEL 6:10 KJV

Know Any Mean Girls?

Have you ever known a mean girl?
Have you ever been accused of being a mean girl?

Mean girls can set the tone for your whole school experience. Get on their bad side, and your days can be filled with pure misery.

Bullying is actually an act of jealousy. People always seem to want to be the best at everything they do. And when they fail, they try to take attention off themselves by picking on someone else. To call a smart kid a cheater might in some way make the bully feel clever. To call a girl ugly and fat might make a mean girl feel prettier. Rather strange, but true.

A nursery rhyme says, "Words can't hurt me," but that's false. Words can cut very deep.

We need to talk about this kind of hurt that is done to us. But even if at first you feel you can't talk to your parents or a friend, Jesus is listening. He sees what is happening to you and how it makes you feel. He understands because He was victim of the ultimate unjust act of bullying (read Mark 14 and 15).

Whisper of Wisdom

Bread a man gets by lying is sweet to him,
but later his mouth will be filled with sand.
Proverbs 20:17 NLV

I've Got the Joy, Joy, Joy. . .

When you are filled with joy, it will spill over to those around you. They will see Christ in you before you even say a word!

Have you ever sung the song about having the joy "down in my heart"? What exactly does that mean? Do we, as Christians, have to walk around with smiles on our faces all the time? Are we supposed to be happy that bad things happen to us? No, God doesn't require that we have a permanent smile, nor does He expect us to be happy when bad things happen.

God is the source of true joy. When bad things happen, remember the joy of Christ. His love and provision for you can give you strength to make it through even the worst of times. You don't have to rejoice because of the difficulty, but you can rejoice in God during the hard times and know that He will help you make it through.

Thank God for His joy today—and share that joy with others!

Whisper of Wisdom

I have told you these things, that My joy and delight may be in you, and that your joy and gladness may be of full measure and complete and overflowing.

JOHN 15:11 AMP

The Diving Board

As you plunge into womanhood,
God is here to help.

Josie's heart pounded as she inched to the end of the diving board suspended high above the public pool. In all of her twelve years, she'd never had the nerve to jump off the high dive.

"Go on!" the older girl behind her urged.

Josie's eyes darted around the pool beneath her. Children played in the shallow end, parents chatted on striped chairs, and clusters of teenagers giggled, all oblivious to the frightening ordeal Josie faced above their heads.

"We don't have all day!" The impatient teenager crossed her arms.

Josie suddenly felt exposed and self-conscious of her developing body in her bathing suit: no longer a little girl but not yet a woman. Oh, how she wished she had never climbed that ladder!

"Jump or get off!"

Josie realized that this diving board was much like her life: She was poised on the brink of womanhood, gathering the nerve to jump in with both feet. It was a scary place she'd never been before, and she knew she didn't have enough strength on her own.

"Lord," Josie whispered, "I trust You, and I know You'll catch me." She felt peace fill her heart. Then she took a deep breath and jumped.

Whisper of Wisdom

Instead of worrying, pray.

PHILIPPIANS 4:6 MSG

"My Parents Drive Me Crazy!"

Children are to honor their parents and obey them in all things.
Your parents have your best interests at heart.

You might feel as though your parents only want to make you crazy with all of their rules and boring limitations. It would be so great to have the freedom that some of your friends have, wouldn't it? The thing is, your mom and dad are doing their job and honoring God in their role as parents. If they lightened up on the reins and gave you more freedom, allowing you to do things that were not in your best interest, they would be going against God's wishes for them.

The main reason your parents are tough on you is that their one goal is to train you now, while you're under their roof, so that when you are an adult, you'll remember the things you learned as a child. It's important for it to happen this way so that you can pass the same training on to your own child. It's God's way. Your parents didn't design it to be that way. So honoring your parents as they follow God's plan is like honoring God Himself.

Whisper of Wisdom

Train up a child in the way he should go,
and when he is old he will not depart from it.
PROVERBS 22:6 NKJV

Be Bold

God has given you the tools to do amazing things.
Use these gifts to bring honor to Him.

It feels great to be good at something. Whether it's kicking a soccer ball, singing a song, playing an instrument, writing poetry, listening to a friend, giving a speech, or teaching little kids, our natural abilities are gifts from God.

Some talents seem to be easier to use to bring honor to God. Singers join the church choir and musicians play on the praise team. Natural teachers lead a Sunday school class, while public speakers prepare devotions for youth group. But the truth is that every gift from God can be used for His glory.

Soccer players can share Jesus with non-Christians on the field. Poets can write God's encouragement to people who need it. Good listeners help others get through difficult times.

Whatever your talents are, share them with others. If you don't know what your gifts are, ask God to reveal them to you. Your heavenly Father is proud of everything you accomplish for His glory.

Whisper of Wisdom

Become the kind of container God can use to present
any and every kind of gift to his guests for their blessing.
2 Timothy 2:20 MSG

Ready. . .Aim. . .Fire!

It's easy to start a war. But how do you make peace?

Do you have a pesky brother or sister? A schoolmate who drives you crazy? Does being around him or her make you want to pull your hair out?

Some people are difficult to deal with, and it's true that you can't do much about their actions. But you *can* control the way you react to them. As a child of God, you are called to be a *peacemaker*.

Getting along with others isn't always easy, especially if someone is determined to have her own way. But treating that person the way they are treating you will only add fuel to the fire. Making peace means going out of *your* way to get along. Try letting your pesky brother have the last cookie, or try volunteering to do the dishes when it's his turn. Say something nice to that hard-to-deal-with schoolmate. Be a friend to the unfriendly.

A little extra kindness may be all it takes to end the feud between you and your brother or sister. And that annoying schoolmate might turn out to be a great pal. Best of all, you'll earn the reputation—on earth and in heaven—as a peacemaker.

Whisper of Wisdom

Blessed are the peacemakers:
for they shall be called the children of God.

MATTHEW 5:9 KJV

Reading the Fine Print

Learning somebody's name doesn't tell you everything about them—how about learning what's behind the name?

If your mom keeps a cleaning solution under the kitchen sink, take a minute to look at its label. Besides the directions for using it, there's probably a warning label about *mis*using it. It's important to heed such words of caution.

But you know what? It's even *more* important to pay attention to God's words of caution about misusing His holy name.

His warning label is posted in the Ten Commandments and states that it's serious business for His people to throw His name around as they please. God's name is sacred and too special to speak carelessly. Just as you wouldn't wear your best outfit to play mud volleyball, so God doesn't want someone dragging His name through the dirt. His holy name doesn't fit in the same sentence with words of anger aimed at someone else.

Be wise, princess, in how you use God's name. Instead of tossing it around carelessly, treat it as the special treasure it is. That's a label worth reading!

Whisper of Wisdom

Do not misuse the name of the LORD your God.
EXODUS 20:7 HCSB

Confession Obsession

Wish you could feel better? Ease that heavy burden?
Deal with the ache in your heart?

*T*ry confession! It's good for the soul. To confess something means you admit it to someone. You tell what you've done—even if it's really, really hard.

Need an example? Imagine you've done something bad. Really bad—like stolen a pack of chewing gum from the drugstore or cheated on a test at school or blabbed one friend's secret to impress another friend. You haven't told anyone about it—you wouldn't dare. If people knew, it would change the way they think about you. And besides, some secrets are okay to keep, right?

Wrong. According to the verse below, it's better to just get it off your chest. Tell someone. And don't give them the watered-down version, either. Tell them the whole ugly story, even the parts that are the hardest to share. Afterward, ask them to pray for you so that you will be stronger the next time you're tempted.

There, now! Doesn't that feel better? Feel that weight lifted? Confessing your sins is good for you! And your friends will respect you for being so open and honest.

Whisper of Wisdom

Make this your common practice: Confess your sins to each other and pray for each other so that you can live together whole and healed. The prayer of a person living right with God is something powerful to be reckoned with.

JAMES 5:16 MSG

When No One Is Looking

The woman you become is determined by what you do when you think no one is looking. Choices made in secret can create a lasting reputation.

It feels so good to be liked! But if someone wants you to talk badly about your friend, even when she may never know, your choice may be a defining moment. Will you become known as a loyal friend who upholds her friend's honor? Or will you build a reputation as one who is easily swayed into giving up her loyalties just to gain the favor of someone else?

This goes for all areas of life. Will you obey your parents when they aren't around and grow into an obedient, trustworthy person? Will you respect your teachers by doing your own work rather than cheating so that you can build a reputation of honesty for yourself? A good reputation must be built, and it even includes the things you do when no one is looking—because even when no one else sees, God sees the good that you do, and He will reward you for it.

Whisper of Wisdom

"Then your Father, who sees what is done in secret, will reward you."

MATTHEW 6:4 NIV

Think, Then Speak

It's important to think first and then speak.
Things just work better that way!

Have you heard the saying "Say what you mean, and mean what you say"? Sometimes words come out before you think them through. It can be because you're distracted, or sometimes it just seems easier to agree with someone else rather than say what's really on your mind. But both scenarios can lead to trouble.

Just imagine. . .you're at the best part in your book, or your favorite TV show is just coming on. Your little brother or sister comes and asks you to play. You answer, "I will in just a few minutes." But you know you have a book report due tomorrow and it will take all of the time you have left in the day. Before you know it, your brother or sister is in tears and has told your parents all about it, and you find yourself frustrated—with that book report still due tomorrow.

Before agreeing to something, take a moment to think it through. Jesus has said to just give a simple answer—and His way is always best.

Whisper of Wisdom

"Just say a simple, 'Yes, I will,'
or 'No, I won't.'"
MATTHEW 5:37 NLT

Realistic Expectations

Expect your greatest reward to come from God—not others.

*T*he Bible says you are to love those who aren't nice to you, be good to them, and lend to them—all without expecting anything in return. Sounds hard, doesn't it?

Imagine if Lucy took the last piece of delicious cake that you thought you were going to share. And to top it off, it's your favorite dessert—chocolate cake with peanut butter icing! Argh! The easiest thing to do would be to snatch the cake out of her hand, yell at her, and gulp it down before she has a chance to grab it back. But that's not what God wants you to do. Instead of you swallowing that cake, He wants you to smile at Lucy and ask her if she'd like some nice cold milk with her dessert!

It's not always easy to be nice when other people aren't, but you must try to love everyone—no matter what. And when it seems too hard to do, remember to pray and ask God's help to love them and treat them the way He wants you to—without expecting anything in return from them.

If you do what God asks, your reward from Him will be great, because then you are showing Him and others that you are God's princess.

Whisper of Wisdom

"Love your enemies, do good to them, and lend to them
without expecting to get anything back. Then your reward
will be great, and you will be sons of the Most High,
because he is kind to the ungrateful and wicked."

Luke 6:35 NIV

No Fear

Does something or someone have your knees knocking?
Not anymore! You don't have to be afraid!

Are you secretly afraid of someone or something? Maybe it's a mean person at school, or maybe you're still afraid of the dark and you don't want anyone to ever find out. It's okay to admit you're afraid. And guess what—you can do something about it!

The next time fear creeps up on you, repeat this verse: "The Lord is my helper, I will not be afraid." The Bible tells us in 1 John 4:18 that "perfect love drives out fear" (NIV). That is another great verse to memorize and repeat when you are scared.

Remember that being afraid is not uncommon. To tell you the truth, a lot of adults are scared of something, too! But you have a weapon, a sword of light, to help you fight off the darkness. That weapon is Jesus!

Just remember that Jesus, your Light, is always with you, and you can get through the darkest, scariest moments knowing that He is right by your side.

Whisper of Wisdom

So we say with confidence, "The Lord is my helper;
I will not be afraid. What can man do to me?"

HEBREWS 13:6 NIV

Light of Mine

Jesus is a light in your life.
Use His light to help others find their way.

The Sunday school class stared up at the teacher as she droned on about the bloodline of Jesus. Thunder rumbled outside the church. *Could the lesson be any more boring?* they wondered.

Suddenly the power went out and the room was plunged into darkness. Everyone panicked. A few students even yelled out in alarm. After a few moments of chaos, the teacher flicked on a flashlight that illuminated her corner of the room. The students quickly settled back into their seats as their eyes adjusted to the light.

"How did the darkness make you feel?" the teacher asked.

"Scared and confused—like I was alone all of a sudden," one student said.

"That's how the world feels without Jesus," the teacher said. "But the light from my flashlight offers reassurance and hope. Jesus is an even greater light inside you. Don't hide that light from others when you know they need the same joy you have in Christ."

Whisper of Wisdom

"You are the light of the world. . . . Let your light shine before men, that they may see your good deeds and praise your Father in heaven."

MATTHEW 5:14, 16 NIV

The Company You Keep

*Choose your friends wisely, because you
will become like the company you keep.*

Young girls often try to fool themselves (and their parents) into believing that they won't be influenced by the bad behavior of others. So eager to fit in, they will deny the fact that the language, activities, and behaviors of their friends will have an influence on them.

Jesus doesn't ask His children to isolate themselves. In fact, He wants us to be part of the world around us. But we should be shaping the world, not letting the world shape us.

We can only impact the world when we strive to be "joined" or united solely with people who share our love for Jesus and our goal of pleasing Him with our lifestyle. If you feel that these types of people are difficult to find, pray that God will lead you to ones who will build you up and with whom you can live as an example to others.

To stay in God's light, ask Him to give you wisdom in choosing your friends.

Whisper of Wisdom

Do not be joined together with those who do not belong to Christ. How can that which is good get along with that which is bad? How can light be in the same place with darkness?

2 Corinthians 6:14 NLV

Service with a Smile

Bring a smile to someone's face. It will bring one to your own. Serve others with gladness.

Chloe looked at the table where her brother Zach sat. His backpack was open, and his school supplies were strewn about. She could tell it would be awhile before his homework was completed. She also knew that Zach's barn chores were still waiting. If he had to do all that homework and all the barn work, he'd never have time to watch the baseball game he'd so much been looking forward to.

Chloe didn't care much for the jobs she knew were waiting, but she loved her brother, and she wanted to help. She quietly left the house. An hour later, Chloe came back inside. As Zach finished his math assignment, his sister popped a bag of popcorn. It was time for the game to start.

"Are you coming?" Chloe called into the dining room, a big grin on her face.

"I still have to. . ." Zach stopped as he realized what Chloe's smile meant. "You're the best!" he exclaimed as he jumped up from the table and bear-hugged her.

Chloe beamed. Mucking the stalls was worth it.

Whisper of Wisdom

The Son of man came not to be ministered unto, but to minister, and to give his life a ransom for many.

MATTHEW 20:28 KJV

Listen, My Child

Listen up! Pay attention! Focus!

*H*as this ever happened? You're focused on a television show or a video game and your mom is trying to talk to you. You hear her. Sort of. But you're not really paying attention. Why? Because your mind is on other things. You're distracted.

Listen up, princess! To really listen means you're focused on what's being said to you. You're not planning your next slumber party or thinking about who you're going to the mall with. You're not watching your favorite TV show or sending a text message to someone. When you're really listening, you hear everything the other person says. Every single word. You're giving them your full, undivided attention, and you're doing it because you care about what they're saying.

You have so much to learn from the adults in your life. When your parents ask for your attention, it's often because they're trying to teach you something. The best way you can show them you're learning is to do what they say. In other words, to listen means to obey. So listen up!

Whisper of Wisdom

Listen, my son, to your father's instruction and do not forsake your mother's teaching. They will be a garland to grace your head and a chain to adorn your neck.

PROVERBS 1:8-9 NIV

More or Less

Happiness is being content with what we have.

A horn beeped and arms waved as the shiny red convertible zipped past two backpack-bent girls trudging along the sidewalk.

"Wow—looks like Gigi's mom got a new car." Twelve-year-old Lynn waved halfheartedly at the red blur disappearing around the bend. "Again."

"Oooh, it's even prettier than the last one!" little Marilee gushed, waving both hands. "Why don't we ever get a new car, Lynn?"

Lynn glanced at her first-grade sister's innocent blue eyes. She didn't know she was poor.

"Well, Marilee, it's just that our old car still has some life in it yet, and it would be a shame not to let it live out all its days."

"Is that why Dad takes it apart and puts it back together so much?"

"Yep." Lynn smiled and tousled her little sister's golden curls. She had learned to be satisfied with what she had, not make herself miserable wishing for what she didn't. "Our family's all about long life. Why, nobody gets as many miles out of sneakers as we do; our washing machine is as old as Grandma, and our hand-me-downs never die!"

Marilee grinned. "And we have the happiest house in town."

Whisper of Wisdom

I know how to get along with little and how to live when I have much. I have learned the secret of being happy at all times.

PHILIPPIANS 4:12 NLV

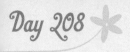

Between Sundays

Do you learn enough about Jesus on Sunday to last you all week long? Do you have an adult to look up to Monday through Saturday?

Sundays are special days to get together with other Christians to worship God and study the Bible, but it's the things we learn and the decisions we make during the week that make all the difference in life.

Jesus taught through stories how God's ways are important for everyday life—not just for Sundays. God has a way of making everyday things—like arguments with a sibling, bullying in the school hallway, and struggles in team practice—easier, if we are willing to learn.

Much can be discovered through reading your Bible, but God also designed life so that we can learn from other Christians how we should react in different situations.

If you have Christian parents, watch them and ask them for advice. If you have not been blessed with Christian parents, ask a pastor or Sunday school teacher for help finding a mentor. Many Christian adults are happy to take time to help you learn God's ways.

Whisper of Wisdom

Teach them to your children, talking about them when you sit at home and when you walk along the road, when you lie down and when you get up.

DEUTERONOMY 11:19 NIV

The Princess Priority

*Hey, what about sliding your feet into your shoes
and then putting on your socks? Some things
just have to be done in the right order.*

If a friend took money from your wallet to buy you a birthday gift, would you be impressed with her kindness and generosity? Would anybody try to do that to God and get away with it?

Well, ask Saul, the first king of Israel. He might say, "Yes, I thought I could fool God. You see, after my military victory, God told me to keep my hands off the loot, but I didn't listen because I wanted to take the best stuff for myself. Well, the prophet Samuel caught me red-handed as I was offering up to God some of my stolen goods."

So what does God think of such a scheme? God desires His princess to remember that obedience is the first priority. If you forget which comes first, check the dictionary, where obedience always comes before sacrifice.

Whisper of Wisdom

*"What is more pleasing to the LORD: your burnt offerings
and sacrifices or your obedience to his voice?"*
1 SAMUEL 15:22 NLT

You Are a Masterpiece

As the master artist, God signed His name on
the canvas of your life. You make Him proud.

The moment God created you, He smiled. Only the master artist could create a person whose eyes can see more than ten million different colors and whose body parts function so perfectly together. He knows every hair on your head—even though you shed dozens of them every day—and every millimeter your toenails grow. He knows each of the forty million times your heart will beat this year and can identify each one of the more than two trillion red blood cells pumping through your circulatory system right now.

As proud as God was when He thought you into existence, He's even more pleased when you ask Him to make you new again by accepting Jesus Christ. That's when you—the masterpiece of His creation—become a sinless and perfected version of yourself through the grace offered by Jesus' death and resurrection.

Think of it—you're a priceless masterpiece times two! God has a wonderful future planned for His children—both here on earth and in eternity in heaven.

Whisper of Wisdom

For we are God's masterpiece. He has created
us anew in Christ Jesus, so we can do the
good things he planned for us long ago.
EPHESIANS 2:10 NLT

Listen Up!

Wanted: A princess who is quick to listen, slow to speak, and slow to get mad. (Know anyone like that?)

Are you one of those girls who loves to be the center of attention? Maybe you like to be the one doing all of the talking, interrupting others when it's not really your turn. Well, listen up! The Bible says that God's daughters need to be quick to listen and slow to speak. That means you have to be silent long enough to pay attention to what others are saying.

So how about it, princess? Is it hard for you to be quiet when others are talking? And what happens when your feelings get hurt? Do you spout off, like a teakettle boiling over? Do the words come flying out of your mouth? Do you wish you could take them back afterward?

It's hard to un-say something, isn't it? Better not to say it in the first place! So take a deep breath and count to three. Don't speak without carefully thinking about what you're going to say. And remember that God's girls are quick to listen!

Whisper of Wisdom

Understand this, my dear brothers and sisters: You must all be quick to listen, slow to speak, and slow to get angry. Human anger does not produce the righteousness God desires.

JAMES 1:19–20 NLT

Be on Guard

It creeps up on you quietly, but you are ready.
Temptation is no victor this time.

Temptation is all around you every day, and sometimes it can be hard not to stumble and fall into it. A quick glance at your neighbor's test and you'd have a 100 percent—but you'd also have sin on your record. Or what about the new boy in your class who just doesn't quite fit in? All the other kids are making fun of him. Are you tempted to join in the meanness?

In your heart you know the right thing to do. You might even really want to do the right thing, but sometimes it's just so hard. That's why Jesus said to watch and pray. You know you'll face temptation, so be prepared when it comes. Pray daily for strength to resist wrong. Remember also that you'll never face a temptation Jesus didn't face. He never sinned, though, and He's your example. He'll help you be the winner as you face temptation.

Whisper of Wisdom

Watch and pray, that ye enter not into temptation:
the spirit indeed is willing, but the flesh is weak.

Matthew 26:41 KJV

Never Alone

Hello? Is anybody there?

Have you ever felt lonely? Maybe you were the new girl in town and didn't know anyone there. Maybe you had to eat lunch by yourself because you didn't have any friends at school. Remember how you felt? Sad. . .gloomy. . .depressed. But did you know that as a child of God, you are never alone?

God is *always* with you. In school, in your neighborhood, when you're sleeping, eating, playing, or studying. Whether you're having a fantastic day or feeling down in the dumps, He's there!

When you are God's child, He is everywhere you are. He is part of you! You are His own precious daughter, His princess, the apple of His eye. You can talk to your heavenly Father when no one else wants to listen. You can tell Him anything! Your deepest secrets, your wildest dreams, your sorrows and disappointments. He doesn't think you're weird or crazy. You are His special creation, and He adores you.

The next time you feel lonely, whisper a prayer to God and imagine Him sitting right beside you. Because as long as you want Him there, that's where He'll stay—for ever and ever.

Whisper of Wisdom

I am not alone, because the Father is with me.

John 16:32 KJV

Loving Others

Love is the greatest commandment.

*G*od has given us a commandment to love each other as He has loved us. Wow. That's quite a lot. And you know what? It's easy to love those people you like—your best friend, Mom and Dad, your brothers and sisters, and Grandma and Grandpa. But what about the people who don't seem to be very likable—at all? How can you learn to love them?

Well, as God's princess, you know about what God has done for you and how much He loves you. You know He sent His Son to die on a cross for you so that you can have a home in heaven with Him one day. And you know He didn't do it just for you. It was also for all those people who don't seem very lovable.

If you're having a hard time loving someone, ask God for help. Ask Him to let His love shine through you to someone else.

When you do so, you'll be proving to the world that you are God's child—and loving every minute of it!

Whisper of Wisdom

*"So now I am giving you a new commandment:
Love each other. Just as I have loved you, you should
love each other. Your love for one another will prove
to the world that you are my disciples."*

JOHN 13:34-35 NLT

It's Just Stuff

What if you woke up tomorrow. . .
and all of your "stuff" was gone?

Could you live without television? What about computers? The Internet? Cell phones? Video games? Could you manage without your cool shoes, your MP3 player, and your toys? What would you do if all of those things disappeared—never to return? Would your life be harder. . .or easier?

Girls today have lots and lots of "stuff," but some of it keeps us from doing what we should be doing. Imagine you're playing a video game. The hours go by and you don't even realize it. Before long, the whole afternoon has passed. You've missed out on spending time with your family or reading your Bible. You haven't done your homework, and you forgot to write that e-mail to your grandmother that you meant to write.

See how our "stuff" gets in the way? And here's the problem: We think we can't live without it. Here's a fun challenge: For one full day, give it up! Don't think you can do it? Give it a try, princess! After all. . .it's just stuff!

Whisper of Wisdom

Do not love the world or anything in the world.
If anyone loves the world, the love of the Father is not in him.

1 JOHN 2:15 NIV

My Day Planner

Is your schedule packed with activities?
Don't forget who is in control.

Birthday parties, sleepovers, sports, piano practice, church, shopping, homework, e-mailing a friend, more homework. . .whew! You are a busy girl! Being busy and having a lot of activities can be fun. But you know what? The devil likes to make us so busy that we forget to spend time with God.

All of our activities are fine and good as long as we are keeping God first in our life and not cramming so much into our schedule that we never have time to go to church or pray or read our Bibles. Feel like you don't have any control over your busy schedule? Talk to your parents and ask them to help you with your priorities. Make a list of what you have to do and what you want to do. Pray and ask the Lord to help you decide what is most important. Remember who is in control, and let God be your "Day Planner."

Whisper of Wisdom

You can make many plans,
but the Lord's purpose will prevail.
PROVERBS 19:21 NLT

Approach the Throne

God eagerly waits for you to come meet Him at His throne.
His arms are open wide to you.

Many kings in the Old Testament held all the power—especially in their throne rooms. Advisers, subjects, and even family members were not allowed to come into the king's presence unless invited by the king himself. Anyone who chanced it and approached the throne without invitation ran the risk of a death sentence.

Some people think God is just as unreachable as the ancient kings, believing that since He lives in heaven and for now we're here on earth, His children are kept outside of His presence.

The truth is that Jesus opened the door to God's throne room by giving up His life on the cross. The invitation is open to everyone who accepts. Through prayer, worship, praise, thankfulness, study of His Word, and time spent with other Christians, we enter God's presence. Talk to Him. Open up your heart to Him. He's a King who not only welcomes you into His presence but opens up His arms to greet you.

Whisper of Wisdom

Because of Christ and our faith in him, we can now
come boldly and confidently into God's presence.

EPHESIANS 3:12 NLT

Waiting at the Princess Crossing

If it doesn't seem cool to wait at the intersection, then consider the alternative—that's really not cool.

When you were younger, your parents or other adults probably often reminded you to stand still on the curb until it was safe to cross a busy street. They didn't want you to run out into traffic. God feels that way about His princess standing on the edge of temptation.

The devil loves to convince you it's safe to dash out, for example, and grab something you like from someone else. Instead, God asks you to stand firmly on the curb, waiting for Him to supply your need. No need to harm yourself by running headfirst into disobedience. Like those standing with you at the curb, God desires to keep you safe by having you follow His lead.

So before dashing out into unsafe territory, take hold of God's hand and wait for Him. That's the cool—and smart—thing to do.

Whisper of Wisdom

*Stay alert! Watch out for your great enemy, the devil. . . .
Stand firm against him, and be strong in your faith.*

1 Peter 5:8-9 nlt

Control Your Thoughts

Jesus gives us wisdom about what is right and conviction to know what is wrong. Don't allow the negative to take over your thoughts, because it will run your life.

Satan uses all sorts of methods to get control of your thoughts. Like when a friend talks negatively about your parents, or another friend convinces you that you shouldn't study, or someone else tries to make you believe that church is boring. Slowly, if you allow those negative voices to continue, those thoughts will begin to creep into your life, turning you from what is good and causing you to focus on what is bad for you.

Take control of your thoughts by allowing only positive things and people who support what is right for you into your life. Avoid cynical and sarcastic friends who only want to see you turn from good and run toward evil.

Let the words of wisdom and the encouragement of mature believers guide the way you see the world. Since your thoughts will run your life, make sure your thoughts are of the things of God.

Whisper of Wisdom

*Be careful what you think,
because your thoughts run your life.*
PROVERBS 4:23 NCV

In Christ's Name

What kinds of things are you praying for?
Are your desires appropriate?
Will God be glorified?

I just don't get it," Kaitlyn complained. "I've been praying for a new iPod, and God isn't listening."

Kaitlyn's mother smiled. This wasn't the first time they'd had this conversation. "Kait, just because you didn't get an iPod doesn't mean God's not listening. Maybe He's telling you to wait, or maybe He's telling you no."

"But the Bible says that if I ask in Jesus' name, I'll receive what I ask for. I always say, 'In Jesus' name,' " she said.

"It seems you're using that verse and those words as a magic formula," said her mother. "The real meaning of that verse is that you should be walking so close to Jesus that your desires are His desires. You will pray for things that bring glory to God. It doesn't mean you shouldn't have the iPod. It just means you need to think about what's really important."

Kaitlyn understood her mom's meaning. She'd keep praying about the iPod, but she'd be sure her attitude was the right one.

Whisper of Wisdom

Whatsoever ye shall ask in my name, that will I do,
that the Father may be glorified in the Son.

JOHN 14:13 KJV

Wardrobe Check!

Jeans, T-shirt, tennis shoes. . .love?

*H*ave you ever had one of those mornings when you just couldn't decide what to wear? Maybe you picked out one outfit, put it on, then decided to wear something else. Once you looked in the mirror, you weren't happy with that outfit, either. Before long everything ended up in a pile on the floor and you still weren't sure what to wear.

Decisions, decisions. What you wear is important to you, but one item in your wardrobe is especially important to God! Reach way back into your closet (or into your drawer) and pull out. . .love! Slip it over each shoulder. Wrap it around your heart. There. . .doesn't that feel nice? It's by far the prettiest thing you can put on!

Seem a little silly? It's not. Wear love like you would wear a warm, fuzzy jacket. Let it surround you on every side so that when you bump into people—and you surely will—God's love will rub off on them, too! Slip it over your head like a winter cap so that your thoughts are always His thoughts.

Love—now that's one attractive outfit!

Whisper of Wisdom

Even more than all this, clothe yourself in love.
Love is what holds you all together in perfect unity.
Colossians 3:14 NCV

Spirit Perfume

Do you like fruity-or flowery-smelling lotions and perfumes?
Have you known a person who wears so much of a certain scent
that the smell lingers even after she has left the room?

*D*id you know that you have an odor? Not just after dance class or a soccer game.

The Bible tells us our spirit has a fragrance that God can smell and that even affects the people around us. The more we keep a good attitude, an unselfish manner, and a serving heart about us, the more the fragrance of godliness surrounds our spirit—that part of us that lives on forever. But if your attitude is full of bitterness and selfishness, the odor of your spirit is going to be unpleasing and push others away.

So just as you dab on lotion or perfume each morning, check that you are putting on a pleasant perfume in your spirit. You want to be able to leave the room and have others say, "She smelled good, just like a child of God."

Whisper of Wisdom

We are a sweet smell of Christ that reaches up to God.
It reaches out to those who are being saved from the
punishment of sin and to those who are still lost in sin.

2 CORINTHIANS 2:15 NLV

Feet First

When you walk, you get to your destination one step at a time.
The next time, count your steps.

If you play a musical instrument, someday you might decide to join a marching band. That's when you'll make the amazing discovery that not only must your fingers be on the right keys, but your feet have to be in the right place. How do you learn to keep in step with the Drum Major in God's marching band?

Instead of getting your feet all tangled up in anger, jealousy, greed, and the like, allow God to put you in step with His love, joy, peace, and patience. Following God's lead gives your step a "super"natural rhythm of grace and beauty, but focusing on your missteps will easily discourage you.

Naturally you'll lose your concentration sometimes, but the Drum Major will always help you get back in step. God's just glad to have you marching with Him.

Whisper of Wisdom

Since we are living by the Spirit, let us follow the
Spirit's leading in every part of our lives.
GALATIANS 5:25 NLT

A Witness for Jesus

There are many people in the world who have not heard about Jesus. When they observe the way you live, will they see Him?

Every day, we come in contact with many people. Have you ever wondered how many of them actually know Jesus? We tend to think that in the United States, everyone has heard about Jesus. But that isn't true. There are a great number of people in our country who haven't heard about God's love for them.

Each of us should be ready to share our faith with others, but we should also be living each day so that they can see Jesus in us. If we are dishonest, or use bad language, or cheat, do you think they'll want to know the same Jesus we claim to love? Will they see any difference in us than in their friends who aren't Christians?

Take a look inside yourself and see if there are any changes you need to make in your behavior so that you can be a better witness for Him.

Whisper of Wisdom

For you will be His witness unto all men of everything that you have seen and heard.

Acts 22:15 AMP

Obsession

*Some people can name every fact about their favorite celebrities.
God knows even more about you.*

Celebrity gossip magazines, entertainment TV shows, and websites supply every little-known fact we can imagine about people in the spotlight. Fans can find out the preferred lip gloss, jeans brand, and coffee drink of their favorite singers, actors, celebutantes, and reality TV stars.

Some fans research the biography of their favorite celebrity, memorizing facts about their childhood and family. Although it may seem silly to someone on the outside, to a fan, even the most boring fact seems important.

God's love for and interest in you run even deeper than the interest of an obsessed fan. He cares so much for you that He knows every fact about you that nobody—even you—knows, like how many hairs are on your head at this very moment. He knows every thought you think, every emotion you feel, every action you take.

If God cares to know you so intimately, just think about how valuable you are to Him! The next time you wish for the bright lights of celebrity, remember that God's love for you is far deeper than fan obsession.

Whisper of Wisdom

"What is the price of five sparrows—two copper coins? Yet God does not forget a single one of them. And the very hairs on your head are all numbered. So don't be afraid; you are more valuable to God than a whole flock of sparrows."

LUKE 12:6-7 NLT

More Than Just a Building

Church may meet at a building, but it is far more than just a structure with a roof. It is made up of the family of God, who wants His children to meet together often.

Lots of activities come up on the weekends, and they always seem to conflict with church. A sleepover at a friend's house, a day at the beach, or a trip to an amusement park may promise to be great fun. But such temptations are really a deception of Satan, who wants you to believe that it's acceptable to skip church for reasons like these.

Satan wants to separate the people of God from each other because we are strengthened when we are together. God designed it so that we would build each other up and unite with a spiritual bond that cannot be re-created outside of the church. It's true that you can worship God anywhere. But He knows you need the encouragement and warmth of fellowship with other Christians. You need the help you can get from studying God's Word with others and from praying with them. Be faithful in meeting with God's people each week.

Whisper of Wisdom

Let us not give up meeting together, as some are in the habit of doing, but let us encourage one another.
HEBREWS 10:25 NIV

My Idol

*What is an idol? Whom or what do you idolize?
Is the word "idol" pleasing to God?*

TV shows hold contests to pick the best singer, survivalist, cook, designer, model, businessperson, even bride in the land. Every viewer judges them, looking for the very best qualities that stand out above all others. But the winner's moment of fame is often that—a moment—and soon we've forgotten his or her name.

An idol is anything in your life that is held up above God or that gets more of your attention than God.

God is firm when He tells us that we are to put nothing before Him. No person, nothing you own, no hobby or activity you enjoy should ever push God out of first place in your life. He should be the first Friend you call, the last One you talk to at night, your most prized possession, and your biggest insurance toward a positive future.

Each day be sure to check what you are giving first place and work to keep God at the top of the list.

Whisper of Wisdom

Little children, keep yourselves from idols.

1 JOHN 5:21 KJV

Road Trip

*Like a map helps us find our way,
the Bible is our life map.*

"So what's your brother doing now?" Larissa's voice asked over the phone receiver.

"He's stuck like glue to that computer monitor, just like he always is when Mom and Dad are away." Brittany shifted the phone to her left ear as she rolled onto her back and sprawled across her bed. "I can't believe they actually leave him in charge."

"Well, they can't leave you in charge—you're only ten, and he's fourteen!"

"Yeah, but even I understand why Dad puts limits on our computer time. I might want to break the rules, too, but I know I need to have a little self-control and not let myself get lost in cyberspace. I want to be in control of me, not some computer game."

"Self-control—now that's something I need to work on." Larissa sighed.

"Doesn't everybody?" Brittany slid to the floor. "I think we have to figure out what God wants for us, head in that direction, and don't stop until we get there. Then we're not tempted to take a lot of side trips."

"Like. . .hang a left into a cyber black hole?"

"Exactly."

Whisper of Wisdom

 Don't get sidetracked; keep your feet from following evil.
PROVERBS 4:27 NLT

Deal or No Deal

Is there something you would give anything to get? Check out what God's Word has to say. Nothing is worth giving up your own soul!

Do you know somebody at church or school who seems to get everything she wants? Do you ever find yourself wishing you were that person?

Many people spend their whole lives trying to make more money so that they can have everything they want. They think that the more "stuff" they have, the happier they will be. The Bible teaches us that it's not worth it to live that kind of life. You end up chasing after earthly pleasures that can never bring you true happiness and losing the real you in the deal. Instead, we should be chasing after God and His will for our lives. Only then can we know true happiness here on this earth and in heaven as well. Give it a try! Deal?

Whisper of Wisdom

"What good would it do to get everything you want and lose you, the real you? What could you ever trade your soul for?"

MARK 8:36 MSG

The Great Pretender

Be true to yourself and others.

Remember Superman? The superhero with X-ray vision, the one who could see through anything? Well, we have someone even more super than that! He's called God!

God can see through anything. He knows what you do and what is in your heart all the time. He knows if you are pretending to care about someone but, in reality, don't like them. He knows when you don't always stand up for what's right. Neither scenario is part of His plan for you.

So what's a princess to do? Turn to Him and ask for some of His superpower. He'll help you learn to love others when you think you can't. He'll give you the strength to stand up for what's right. He'll help you to do these things without pretending–really.

Whisper of Wisdom

Don't just pretend to love others. Really love them.
Hate what is wrong. Hold tightly to what is good.

ROMANS 12:9 NLT

Sloppy Living

Clean your room! Pick up after yourself! Don't be a slob!

If you're a typical girl, you probably get tired of hearing these words, right? Maybe you like to be a little lazy–leave your wrinkled T-shirts wadded up in the corner or forget to make your bed. Maybe your mom's even cool with that.

Well, listen up! It's one thing to leave your clothes on the floor. It's another thing to be sloppy in your spiritual life–forgetting to pray, skipping your Bible reading time. Sometimes we just get busy and forget. Right?

You are a daughter of the King, and your heavenly Father (just like your earthly parents) wants you to learn to be responsible. That means sloppy living isn't cool. Clean up your act, princess! The next time you trip over a pair of dirty socks on the floor, use them as a reminder to pray. And the next time you look at that messy room, remember that God took the time to clean up your mess–your sin– when He sent Jesus, His Son, to die on the cross.

Whisper of Wisdom

You call out to God for help and he helps–he's a good Father that way. But don't forget, he's also a responsible Father, and won't let you get by with sloppy living.

1 PETER 1:17 MSG

A Ticket to Heaven

*Jesus has provided a way for our entrance into heaven.
We don't earn it by our actions or our words. We receive
it freely, by the grace of God, through His Son, Jesus.*

Getting in to see a movie is pretty easy. You just buy a ticket, show it to the ticket taker, select a seat, and enjoy. Without that ticket, though, the ticket taker would have to turn you away from the movie. That ticket proves that you are worthy to enter the movie because you have paid the price for admission.

So it is with heaven. We need a ticket to enter heaven, and the price for that ticket must be paid. At the gates of heaven, we must present our ticket and show that we are worthy to enter. Is it our good works that will make us worthy to enter heaven? No! Can we somehow earn or purchase a ticket to enter heaven? No! There is only one way into heaven, one ticket, and that is through Jesus Christ. He has already bought your ticket and has freely offered it to you. You only need to receive it.

Whisper of Wisdom

*"God loved the world so much that he gave
his one and only Son so that whoever believes
in him may not be lost, but have eternal life."*

JOHN 3:16 NCV

The Lilies of the Field

*Think of your dream outfit. Now imagine a field
of vibrant flowers. Which is truly beautiful to God?*

It's the end of summer, and another school year is upon you. What an exciting time it is! You have the cutest new outfits in mind, and you want to get matching accessories for everything. When you go shopping, reality sets in. Your mom sets the budget and you cringe. How will you ever keep up with the other girls when you're that limited? You'll barely get a new pair of tennis shoes with that amount.

Before you complain, remember that God provides what you really need. He's also the One you really need to think about pleasing with your clothes. Once you accept this truth, consider your options. You don't have to shop at the expensive stores. Inexpensive stores carry nice outfits, and there are some real treasures at thrift shops—especially if you get creative. Why not try those places? You might turn out to be the best-dressed, wisest-spending girl at school.

Whisper of Wisdom

*And why take ye thought for raiment? Consider the
lilies of the field, how they grow; they toil not, neither
do they spin: And yet I say unto you, that even Solomon
in all his glory was not arrayed like one of these.*

MATTHEW 6:28–29 KJV

My Testimony

What do you say when someone asks about your faith?
God wants you to be ready with a loving answer.

Why are you a Christian?

The world wants to know your answer. Maybe you've been asked about your faith before. Did you know what to say? God tells His followers to be prepared to answer anyone who asks us why we believe what we believe.

It's not as scary as it sounds, and it's important to think about your answer before you're asked the question. When someone opens the door for you to share your testimony, talk about your faith in three minutes:

Minute one: Talk about what your life was like and what
struggles you had before you accepted Christ.

Minute two: Share your story of how you became a Christian
and what steps you took to come to that point.

Minute three: Tell about how your life has changed since
beginning a relationship with Jesus and about the hope
you have in spending eternity with Him in heaven.

Your testimony is a special story that is unique to you. It doesn't have to be earth-shattering or tragic to show others the power of Jesus in your life. Your testimony is an amazing recollection of a miracle God performed in you, His child.

Whisper of Wisdom

Always be prepared to give an answer to everyone
who asks you to give the reason for the hope that
you have. But do this with gentleness and respect.

1 PETER 3:15 NIV

The Green-Eyed Monster

Look out! Beware! He's coming after you!

Lurking behind the next corner, a creature is watching, waiting to grab his next victim. His name is Envy, and his purpose is to spread misery and gloom to as many people as possible. If you're not careful, he'll jump on *you*.

"It's not fair!" he'll whisper. "Why does *she* have all of the talent? Why can't you be as pretty as *her*?" Before you know it, you'll be ensnared in his trap, sulking over your best friend's dimples. You'll decide you don't like the spelling bee champion. You'll make fun of the girl who got to sing the solo you wanted. And all the while, you'll become more and more miserable.

Envy wants you to forget who you really are—a child of the heavenly King. He wants you to think that if God really loved you, He would have given *you* those dimples that you like so much. And why didn't He? Because He chose to give you something different. . .something better. . .something just for you.

Tell Envy to scram. You don't need other people's looks or talents or brains. You're terrific just the way you are—the way God created you.

Whisper of Wisdom

Let us not be desirous of vain glory,
provoking one another, envying one another.
GALATIANS 5:26 KJV

Scripture Memorization

God's Word is like a light in a dark world. Knowing it well will give you the tools you need to see clearly in the dark times.

When the lights are off, it's easy to stumble. You can falter in your step, stub your toe, or step on something painful in your efforts to find your way. The same is true when you are in the dark spiritually. God's Word is a lamp that will shine the light onto your path as you walk through life. Its guidance will help you avoid a painful walk through the dark.

Make it a priority to memorize God's Word. Being able to call to mind a scriptural truth and to just know the words of God helps dark things become very clear. The verses you learn will help you when temptation comes your way. They will comfort you through troubled times. They will remind you of how you can please God in your daily life. They are like a light in a dark place. Let God's Word light the way for you in the darkness of the world. Let it shine!

Whisper of Wisdom

Your word is a lamp to my feet and a light for my path.

PSALM 119:105 NIV

A Princess Makes It Her Business

Honesty is not only the best policy—it's God's standard!

What if you find only four sticks of gum when you just paid for a pack of five? Suppose the double-scoop ice-cream cone you ordered has only a single dip on it? Honest mistakes happen, but God despises taking advantage of another person so you can come out ahead.

As God's princess, make it your goal to be honest and accurate when you "do business" with others. Say you owe a friend five dollars. God is delighted when you hand back five dollars but not so happy if you stuff only four bucks in her pocket. Or will you raise your hand if your teacher asks who read the whole chapter when you read only half?

Others will love "doing business" with you when they know you haven't first helped yourself to what they have coming to them. It makes God's day, too.

Whisper of Wisdom

The Lord detests the use of dishonest scales,
but he delights in accurate weights.

PROVERBS 11:1 NLT

D-I-S-C-I-P-L-I-N-E

"I am doing this for your own good. . . ."

How many times have you heard those words from one of your parents? "I'm doing this for your own good." They usually follow them with other words you don't like to hear: "No, you can't spend the night with your friend," or "You have to clean up that messy room!"

Discipline—how we dislike the word. When your parents discipline you, they are taking the time to correct your behavior. Maybe you were supposed to clean up your room days ago, but didn't. Now it's time to pay the piper. You can't spend the night with your best friend, and you've got to stay in there all day, doing what you neglected earlier. Maybe you were rude (or mean) to your little brother, and now you have to do extra chores (fold the clothes or wash the dishes).

Here's the truth: If your parents didn't love you, they wouldn't discipline you. If they didn't give you boundaries, you wouldn't know the difference between right and wrong. And believe it or not, when they use those words—"I'm doing this for your own good!"—they really are!

Whisper of Wisdom

The LORD disciplines those he loves,
as a father the son he delights in.

PROVERBS 3:12 NIV

The Princess Ta-Da!

How many reasons can you think of for doing the same thing twice? Your number one answer is. . .

At the conclusion of the song, the music teacher doesn't hesitate telling the choir to do the whole thing over again. "You're hitting the right notes," he says, "but you're putting no expression into it." Did you know that God isn't keen on hollow notes of praise either? So what can fill them with acceptable praise?

Like the music teacher, God loves to hear praise when you, His princess, put yourself into it. Instead of just going through the motions, God loves to see your eyes light up and hear the enthusiasm in your voice. Then when you tell God how much He means to you and how great He is, He sees it. But most of all, God is pleased when your praise comes from your heart. Now, that's a ta-da moment!

When you open your mouth with praise like that, God may ask you to do it again, just because it was too beautiful to do only once.

Whisper of Wisdom

My whole being will exclaim,
"Who is like you, O Lord?"
PSALM 35:10 NIV

Heart Beauty

When God looks at you, He doesn't see your physical beauty.
You may be gorgeous by the world's standards,
but God wants your heart to be beautiful.

LouAnne was the girl in school who got picked on the most. With her straggly brown hair, face full of freckles, thick glasses, knobby knees, and crooked teeth, she seemed the perfect target for teasing.

Every day she'd walk through the hallways of her junior high, dodging the jeers of her classmates. "Hey, LouAnne, are those your legs, or are you sitting on a chicken?" "LouAnne, don't you own a comb?" "Snaggletooth, get some braces, will you?"

LouAnne spent her fourth-period study halls helping in a special education classroom. One day she worked with Dirk, a student with Down syndrome, on his homework.

"Dirk, you're doing so well!" LouAnne said as he finished his first worksheet. "I'm proud of you."

Dirk grinned and then turned serious.

"Lou," Dirk said, "I hear kids say stuff about how you look."

"Yeah," LouAnne replied, suddenly feeling uncomfortable.

"Don't listen to them," Dirk whispered. "'Cause I think you're pretty. So does God. Pretty on the outside and in here." He pointed to her heart.

Whisper of Wisdom

"The Lord doesn't see things the way you see them. People judge by outward appearance, but the Lord looks at the heart."
1 Samuel 16:7 NLT

What Jesus Says

Love each other.

You know Jesus wants you to love others. But what about those you find hard to love, much less like?

Hmm. How do you treat an "unlikable"? Well, first off, do nothing that would hurt her. That means you shouldn't gossip about her or try to embarrass her. And here's a good rule to remember: If you can't say something good about someone, don't say anything at all. Instead of joining others who are "dissing" someone, stick up for her instead.

The thing about "unlikables" is that you don't know what might have happened to them that makes them hard to like. But maybe if you show concern and care for them, you will find they are much more likable than you first thought.

If you keep the Golden Rule in mind—do unto others as you would have them do unto you—you'll be satisfying God's requirement of loving others. It's that easy!

Whisper of Wisdom

Love does no wrong to others,
so love fulfills the requirements of God's law.
ROMANS 13:10 NLT

Mirror, Mirror

Don't like what you see? Worrying won't change a thing.
You are beautiful just the way you are!

Have you ever stood in front of the mirror for hours, wishing those freckles would disappear or trying to straighten all those curls? Or maybe it's picture day and you woke up with a giant pimple! Do you let your looks change your attitude? Do you let a pimple or a bad hair day get you down?

God's Word tells us in 1 Samuel 16:7 that God looks only at our hearts. You are beautiful just the way God made you, but what really matters is the condition of your heart. It's hard to imagine when you are right in the middle of it, but ten years from now, no one will care if you had to wear glasses during math class. Ask God to help you worry less about what you look like on the outside and more about what your heart looks like on the inside.

Whisper of Wisdom

"Has anyone by fussing before the mirror ever
gotten taller by so much as an inch? If fussing
can't even do that, why fuss at all?"
LUKE 12:25-26 MSG

No Copycats Allowed

*God doesn't want you to look, act, think, and talk like the world.
His plans are far better than anything sin has to offer.*

Can the world look at you and know that you are a Christian?
Being a child of God means more than wearing a Christian T-shirt
and carrying a Bible through the halls of school. God calls us to be
different from the world in the way we talk, act, think, and present
ourselves.

While God does call us to be different, He *doesn't* call us to
be separated from the world. He wants us to interact and have
friendships with people who don't yet know Jesus' love.

Living in Christ means we don't buy this season's must-have
fashions because wearing them would show too much skin. Being
different means making sure our speech avoids bad words, gossip,
and comments that tear others down. Being set apart by God means
seeking out ways to encourage others and giving selflessly to show
God's love.

The world will take notice of the hope and joy true followers of
Christ have. That happiness is something the world longs to have. Be
different and show your friends the way.

Whisper of Wisdom

*Don't copy the behavior and customs of
this world, but let God transform you into a
new person by changing the way you think.*

ROMANS 12:2 NLT

Oops!

You can't believe you just did that!
You feel so bad! What next?

Do you ever wish you had a time machine? A sleek little gadget that could transport you back in time? Back to that moment when you said the wrong thing and hurt a friend's feelings? Back to that day when you really goofed up and upset your parents? To that instant when you made a bad decision and knew that your heavenly Father was less than pleased?

Life is full of mistakes. It's part of being human! But being a child of God means fixing those mistakes as soon as possible. How? Not through time travel, but by being humble. By telling the person you hurt or upset that you're sorry.

God may be disappointed in your bad decision, but He loves it when you humble yourself in prayer and ask for His forgiveness. Your parents may be upset by your goof, but they'll appreciate your apology. Your hurt friend will feel a lot better when she hears you say you're sorry.

Don't putter around in the garage, trying to figure out how to build a time machine. Take the humble route. It works every time.

Whisper of Wisdom

Pride ends in humiliation, while humility brings honor.

Proverbs 29:23 NLT

Flip On the Light Switch

Wow! That light is bright!

Imagine you're in your bedroom late at night and the light is off. You suddenly realize you forgot to do something, so you get out of the bed and tiptoe across the dark room. Along the way, you stub your toe on the edge of the bed, then run smack-dab into the dresser!

Why are you more likely to hurt yourself when the lights are out? Because your vision is limited. There's no light to guide you from one place to another.

It's the same in your Christian life. When the light is turned on, you can see where you're going. But what is the switch that turns on the light? (Are you ready? Bet you're not!) It's love! Yep, love! You've got to turn it on—whether you're at school, with your friends, at the mall, or just hanging out at home with your brothers and sisters. Love is the switch that lights the way, but it's up to you to flip it on!

Whisper of Wisdom

If anyone claims, "I am living in the light," but hates a Christian brother or sister, that person is still living in darkness. Anyone who loves another brother or sister is living in the light and does not cause others to stumble.

1 JOHN 2:9-10 NLT

Just Like Cinderella

Trust and obey God. . .even when it doesn't make sense.

"Where are you taking your best shoes?" Mark asked.

"Um. . .," Julia mumbled. "To Bethany's house."

"Why?"

"I. . .I don't know exactly," Julia stammered. "I was praying and I got this really strong feeling that I should take Bethany my black heels."

Fifteen-year-old Mark shook his head. "You're not making any sense, sis."

"Well, God told a lot of people in the Bible to do things that didn't make sense. He told Noah to build a boat on dry land, and Joshua to win a battle by yelling at a wall. Jesus told His disciples to catch fish by throwing their net on the *other* side of the boat. . .like fish don't swim under *both* sides!"

"And you're supposed to provide the neighbors with footwear?"

"I don't think we have to understand everything God says; we just have to trust Him and obey."

Cradling Julia's shoes with tears in her eyes, Bethany explained that she'd outgrown her only dressy pair and her family couldn't afford more. She'd prayed that somehow God would provide some in time for the banquet night.

"Just like Cinderella!" Julia declared as Bethany's foot slipped into the shoe that fit perfectly.

Whisper of Wisdom

Trust in the LORD with all your heart;
do not depend on your own understanding.

PROVERBS 3:5 NLT

Forget about It!

Your emotions can be hard to manage—especially if you're hurt by something your friend says or does. Forgiving others definitely isn't easy. But when you open your heart and extend forgiveness to someone, you make God happy!

When a friend hurts your feelings, it's likely you will be angry—maybe even a little sad. You might even hold on to your hurt feelings for a while. After all, friends aren't supposed to hurt each other, are they?

No doubt about it, forgiving your friend will be hard. But this could be the perfect opportunity to reflect God's amazing love into the life of someone else—a way for your friend to see God through your actions. After all, God's Word gives us this bit of wisdom: "Dear children, let's not merely say that we love each other; let us show the truth by our actions" (1 John 3:18 NLT).

Talk to God and ask Him to take away your hurt feelings, and then ask Him for His help in extending forgiveness to your friend. And after you forgive her, forget about it. God will be delighted!

Whisper of Wisdom

It's wise to be patient and show what you are like by forgiving others.

PROVERBS 19:11 CEV

Keep Learning

There is comfort in scripture. There is hope in God's Word.
Hide the truth in your heart.

Andrea hit the buzzer and quoted the verse that the emcee indicated. She watched as her points were added to her total. In the end, she was handed the trophy. She'd reached her goal. She'd won the Bible Bee.

Then the speaker for the event came to the podium. "Young people," he said, "we've watched some really smart kids up here onstage tonight. They've worked hard to learn truths from the Bible, and I know God is pleased with them. I hope that everyone here has learned something tonight, but I pray that your learning won't stop here.

"Read God's Word each day. Memorize it. Live by it. God gave it to you so that you might find hope and comfort. Learning it to receive a prize on earth is good, but hiding it in your heart and living by it brings eternal rewards."

Whisper of Wisdom

For whatsoever things were written aforetime
were written for our learning, that we through
patience and comfort of the scriptures might have hope.

ROMANS 15:4 KJV

A Lump of Clay

*God is wanting to mold you into His own very special
work of art. But you must let Him form you as
you follow His direction for your life.*

Have you thought about what you want to do after high school? Are you thinking of going to college? If so, would you want to become a doctor? A lawyer? A teacher? A missionary?

All of those occupations are important. And it's easy to come up with our own plans for our lives, but God is the potter—we are just the clay. The clay doesn't do anything on its own to become a vase or a pot. It just lies on the wheel, waiting for the potter to form it into a very special creation.

Your Potter wants to mold you into a unique creation as well. But in order for you to become that, you need to allow Him to do His work in you. Be willing to do what He wants you to do and go where He wants you to go. Only then will you truly be happy.

Whisper of Wisdom

*So the potter formed [the clay] into another pot,
shaping it as seemed best to him.*

JEREMIAH 18:4 NIV

Hold the Toppings, Princess!

Some things are so naturally appealing, they make a hit by themselves. Serve them up plain and simple!

It's fun to add marshmallows to hot chocolate or drizzle fudge topping over vanilla ice cream, but think twice before piling lies on top of the truth. God is looking for a princess to tell the story straight from the start instead of twisting it to get someone else in trouble.

If you and your sibling get into it with each other, you may be tempted to stir extra details into your story when your parents ask you to explain what happened. It'll go down much better with everyone if you stick to the truth. Why top off the truth with false juicy tidbits? This is your opportunity, princess, to dish up the truth and let it speak for itself.

Whether it's you or your sibling who needs correction, you'll have a clear conscience before God and others about your words. Serving up only the truth means you won't have to cover up any lies with still another story.

Whisper of Wisdom

An honest witness does not deceive,
but a dishonest witness utters lies.

Proverbs 14:5 HCSB

Be Content and Trust God

*End results aren't always clear at the beginning of
a trial you may face. But true trust in God means
that you accept that His will is always for the best,
even when you don't know how the situation will turn out.*

People react to change in one of three ways. Some people are really nervous about every new situation, while others are too full of their own plans to accept what God has for them. And then there are some who are as happy to trust God in the difficult times as they are to rely on Him in the pleasant periods of life.

Has God given you something difficult to face, such as a broken home, a new school, or a class you don't enjoy? Don't be nervous and jittery about your circumstances, waiting for a chance to go a different way. And don't be so full of your own plans that you can't trust God. Learn to be content with His plan. God loves you, and He knows best. Trust Him in all things, and stand strong in the face of change or struggle. True trust reveals itself when things look the worst.

Whisper of Wisdom

"I will make you strong if you quietly trust me."
ISAIAH 30:15 CEV

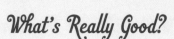

What's Really Good?

Do your actions bring others to Jesus? Does what you do encourage or frustrate? Remember: All that you do affects those around you.

How would you feel if you were walking through your house after dark and suddenly you tripped over a chair that you knew hadn't been there before? You might be angry. You might become frustrated, and you might also get hurt. Stumbling blocks can be a real problem.

Did you know you can be a stumbling block yourself? If your actions cause someone to reject Christ, or if your attitudes discourage someone's Christian growth, you are like that chair in the dark.

The apostle Paul reminds us that just because something isn't sin doesn't mean it's good. He gives the example of eating meat offered to idols. To him it was just meat, and he wasn't worshipping idols. It wasn't sin, but a weaker believer might struggle with idolatry, so if Paul ate the meat, he'd become a stumbling block.

His point is that you need to look at the big picture. How is what you do going to affect others? Don't get in the way of someone's walk with God.

Whisper of Wisdom

*All things are lawful for me, but all things are not expedient:
all things are lawful for me, but all things edify not.*

1 Corinthians 10:23 KJV

Gentle Beauty

What makes someone beautiful? It isn't clothes or makeup or a certain body type. It is what's in the heart.

Who gets to make the decision on beauty, anyway? Throughout the history of the world, women who were considered beautiful have looked drastically different. Women of all body types and skin colors have been classified as beautiful. In thirteenth-century Japanese culture, women were considered beautiful if they had black teeth. Sixteenth-century European women plucked their hairline and scraped their hair back under elaborate headdresses and caked on white makeup to make their skin look pale.

This may sound strange to us today, but some people take extreme measures for beauty: plastic surgery, risky diets, expensive cosmetic products, anti-aging technology, lavish wardrobes, and extravagant jewelry.

God wants His children to look past this outward eye candy. God's standard of beauty starts with a gentle and quiet spirit that displays love, joy, peace, patience, kindness, goodness, and faithfulness. These are the beauty attributes God says will never go out of style.

Whisper of Wisdom

Don't be concerned about the outward beauty of fancy hairstyles, expensive jewelry, or beautiful clothes. You should clothe yourselves instead with the beauty that comes from within, the unfading beauty of a gentle and quiet spirit, which is so precious to God.

1 PETER 3:3-4 NLT

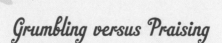

Grumbling versus Praising

The voice of a Christian should be sunny and filled with praise, not full of grumbling and complaining. Our attitudes should always give God glory for the good He has done.

People who always complain aren't very fun to be around. They enjoy being miserable and like to bring other people into that misery by constantly talking about the bad things that happen to them. As Christians, we should never be like that. In all situations, we should think more about the things that went right and the blessings we received. Most of the other stuff isn't worth remembering anyway.

When you're tempted to grumble about something, stop and ask God to help you find a good thing in that situation. Ask Him to show you what good can come from it and to help you learn from each thing that happened.

As followers of Christ, we know that everything comes through the hand of God. So when talking to others, rather than blaming God for the bad things, you should focus on the good things, giving God glory.

Whisper of Wisdom

I will bless the LORD at all times;
His praise shall continually be in my mouth.

PSALM 34:1 NKJV

Clean Your Room!

Don't hide the junk in your life. Get rid of it!

When it's time to clean your room, do you shove everything under the bed? If you've ever tried it, you probably know by now that you can't get away with such tactics for long. Your parents are smart enough to check under that secret place before your room earns a thumbs-up. But have you tried hiding your faults? Disguising the ugly parts of your personality so that no one can see them?

Maybe you're a procrastinator, always putting things off until the last minute. Perhaps you have the bad habit of rolling your eyes or sighing when you're told to do something. These things are faults— areas in your life that need to be cleaned up—just like your bedroom. And rather than trying to hide them in hopes that they won't easily be seen, God expects us to get rid of them.

Throw out the junk in your life. Strive every day to overcome your faults. Confess them to others and ask for their help in getting rid of your bad qualities. Cleaning up your spiritual room is a lot of work, but when you're done, you'll earn a great big thumbs-up from God.

Whisper of Wisdom

Cleanse thou me from secret faults.
PSALM 19:12 KJV

Lay It Down

What does it mean to lay down your life?

When you hear the words "Lay down your life," what do you think of? Does it sound impossible? Laying down your life for someone else is simply a matter of putting them first. It requires sacrifice.

Here's an example. Say you have a grandmother (or great-grandmother) who is very ill. Imagine you're asked to go to her house to care for her. Perhaps you don't want to. Maybe you'd rather hang out with your friends or play video games. But you go because you know you should.

When you arrive, you realize that your grandmother really needs a lot of help. She can't fix her own meals or mop her floors. Why, she even has trouble getting in and out of bed. And she's so happy to see you—so very happy—she begins to cry!

Suddenly, looking into her eyes, you get it. You understand what it means to lay down your life. You will do whatever she needs—not just because it's the right thing to do, but because you love her.

Whisper of Wisdom

This is how we know what love is:
Jesus Christ laid down his life for us. And we
ought to lay down our lives for our brothers.
1 JOHN 3:16 NIV

What's the Greatest?

The greatest thing God wants is for us to love others.

Faith, hope, and love. When asked which was the greatest, Jesus said it was love.

Faith is being sure of what we do not see—God, Jesus, and the Holy Spirit. We show our faith by believing in God's promises, knowing that He will fulfill them because He loves us, and by believing that Jesus is the Son of God who left the Holy Spirit with us to live inside of us.

Hope is having confidence and trust in God, expecting the best from Him. Your hope comes through His love for you. He loves you so much that He brought His only Son to earth to die so that you might have the hope of eternal life with Him in heaven one day.

But love is the greatest of all three. For as God's princess, when you love others and show your love for them, you are living your life the way God wants you to. You are showing your faith in God, in the One who gives us hope.

Whisper of Wisdom

And now these three remain: faith, hope and love.
But the greatest of these is love.
1 CORINTHIANS 13:13 NIV

The Princess Challenge

A long jump takes grit, but a delicate step calls for grace. Are you up for the challenge?

After presenting you with an award, the teacher realizes she made a mistake. You give it up reluctantly and watch a classmate step into the limelight. Awkward move, right? Maybe John the Baptist, a friend and cousin of Jesus, felt that way when curiosity seekers asked him if he was Christ the Messiah.

If people thought John to be the Son of God, he could parade as a star and draw attention to himself. Could John enjoy fooling people for a while? Perhaps somebody else would have tried to steal the show, but John told them straight out he wasn't the Messiah, nor was he a prophet. John told them he was simply the one to prepare the way for the Messiah. In fact, John said he wasn't even worthy to untie Jesus' sandals.

Stepping away from the limelight and celebrating the person who's in the limelight may well be one of the most graceful moves you ever make. Way to go, princess!

Whisper of Wisdom

"I am not the Messiah. . . . I am only someone shouting in the desert, 'Get the road ready for the Lord!'"

JOHN 1:20, 23 CEV

Be a Barnabas!

Be a Barna-what?
Be a Barnabas—an encourager!

*B*arnabas is a man from the Bible who was a friend of Paul. You can read more about him in the book of Acts. He was known for encouraging other people.

It is very important to be an encourager, and there are a lot of people in need of some encouragement! Can you think of some? What about a friend who isn't doing very well in school, or an elderly neighbor or relative who can't get out and about like she used to? Think of ways to brighten up her day. Do you have a friend who has just lost a pet or had someone special move away? You could make him a card to let him know you are thinking about him.

When people think of you, do they think of you as an encourager, or do they think of you as a girl who is down all the time or only thinks about herself? Which would you rather be—one who lifts others up or one who brings others down? Ask God to help you think more about others and to be a better encourager—with all your heart.

Whisper of Wisdom

When he arrived and saw the evidence of the grace of God, he was glad and encouraged them all to remain true to the Lord with all their hearts.

ACTS 11:23 NIV

The Spirit of Intelligence

*Youth are chosen by God to make an extreme
difference in the world and are very important
to the health and growth of the church.*

Respect for your elders is a very important thing. But that
doesn't mean you have nothing to offer just because of your age.
The Holy Spirit moves within each child of God and gives special
understanding of spiritual things. Age is not a boundary or a
limitation with God. So if He gives you something to say or gives you
understanding, don't allow Satan to deceive you into feeling that you
are too young to be taken seriously.

There are many areas of ministry that are great for young
people to get involved in—leading or mentoring those in younger
grades, serving on planning committees for special events, offering
testimonies or prayers at youth events, and so forth. The best thing
you can do for the body of Christ, though, is to have a heart that
desires to bring others to a saving knowledge of Jesus. Invite others
to church and youth events, and learn enough about the Gospel of
Christ so that it becomes easy for you to share it with others.

Whisper of Wisdom

*"I thought, 'Those who are older should speak, for wisdom
comes with age.' But there is a spirit within people, the breath
of the Almighty within them, that makes them intelligent."*

JOB 32:7–8 NLT

Poor and Pure

While you are young, you don't own much of value or have a large bank account. But did you know that right now is when you possess the most valuable thing you will ever own?

Every child is born with it—purity, innocence, and the ability to be shaped by God. And this is a treasure we must work to protect as we grow older.

Nothing—no amount of money in the bank or collection of clothing, electronic gadgets, club memberships, and the like—can bring you greater happiness upon entering adulthood than having your purity untarnished.

Many things in life would like to steal your innocence—books, music, and movies with immoral content; people who want you to try things that God has shown to be wrong; even feelings that make you believe you should have more and be better than others.

Each day you'll encounter things that threaten your body, mind, and soul. Stay on guard. You can tackle each challenge with God's help.

Whisper of Wisdom

A little that a righteous man hath is better than the riches of many wicked.

PSALM 37:16 KJV

Keep a Lid on It

Can others trust you to keep a secret?
God says true friends can keep a confidence.

I didn't mean to tell anybody else that you still suck your thumb when you go to bed," Michaela explained to her friend Jenna. "I'm sorry—I thought it was funny, and if I told somebody else it could be like our little joke."

"A joke at my expense?" Jenna was mad. "Really funny, Michaela. You're nothing but a gossip. See if I ever invite you to another sleepover or share a secret again!" Jenna slammed her locker shut and stormed down the hallway.

Later in study hall, Michaela typed an e-mail to Jenna.

I had no right to tell a secret that you shared with me, Jenna. I'm really sorry. I wouldn't blame you if you never want to talk to me again, but please know that I'm sorry. Michaela

The next day Michaela checked her inbox to find a reply from Jenna.

Michaela, what you did hurt my feelings a lot because you're my friend and you gossiped about me. But I know that God wants me to forgive you, and I do forgive you. See you in gym class.

Jenna

Whisper of Wisdom

A gossip goes around telling secrets,
but those who are trustworthy can keep a confidence.

PROVERBS 11:13 NLT

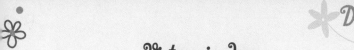
Victory in Jesus

*Look forward to your future.
There is nothing to fear. Through Jesus you are victorious.*

Jillian's eyes were tearful as she said good-bye to her friends. Her father's company had transferred him, and the family was moving to a different town. Not only would she miss her friends, but she was also a bit scared. Her new school would be a lot bigger, and she wouldn't know anyone. What if no one liked her? What if she couldn't find her classroom? So many questions filled her mind.

That night at family devotions, Jillian's dad picked a verse especially for her. "Thanks be to God, which giveth us the victory," he read. Jillian knew that the passage was talking about victory over sin and death, but if Jesus could conquer those for her, certainly He could help her defeat her fears about this big change in her life. God could help her conquer any foe in her life, and she could look forward to each day with confidence.

Whisper of Wisdom

*Thanks be to God, which giveth us the victory
through our Lord Jesus Christ.*
1 CORINTHIANS 15:57 KJV

Lift 'Em Up!

"I'm remembering to lift you up in prayer."

Have you ever been through a really hard time? Going through it alone is tough! Knowing that someone is praying for you really helps.

What if you told your best friend (or maybe one of your parents) what you were going through and asked them to pray for you? Wouldn't that make you feel better? It feels so good to know someone is lifting up your name in prayer. And that works the other way around, too. If you tell someone you're going to be praying for them, they're counting on you to really do it.

But how do you know who to pray for? Try this: Put together a list. Include your family members, and add friends who are going through struggles. Also add people from your church. (Maybe there's an elderly woman in need of prayer or someone with an illness.) Now comes the fun part. Every day (at least once a day), sit down with your list and pray over every name. That's right! Lift up every name! Why, before you know it, you might not even need the list anymore. Lift 'em up, princess!

Whisper of Wisdom

I always thank my God as
I remember you in my prayers.

PHILEMON 4 NIV

Be Watchful

En garde, princess!

In today's world, it's very easy to feel like you are being pulled first one way and then another—because sometimes, you are. But as God's daughter, His princess, you need to stand firm, striving extra hard to be dedicated to doing the things you know are right. That means you must be on your guard against being pulled and going in the wrong direction.

When a fencer is about to battle another swordsman, she says, "En garde!" and assumes a defensive stance. You need to be like that fencer. So, princess, when your friends want you to do things that you know are wrong, no matter how much fun they sound, say, "En garde." Stand ready to fight, to do battle, to resist the temptation to step in the wrong direction. Stand firm in your faith in God, knowing that He will help you stand up for what's right. He'll give you the courage to say no when you want to say yes. And He'll give you the ability to do so in such a way that His love shines through, for you and for them.

Whisper of Wisdom

Be on your guard; stand firm in the faith;
be courageous; be strong. Do everything in love.
1 Corinthians 16:13-14 tniv

"I've Got Your Back"

Watching out for each other is part of friendship.

Rachel didn't know what to do. She could see the outline of the tall man through the window curtain. He had rung the doorbell three times, and now he was knocking. Why wouldn't he go away?

Rachel knew not to open the door to strangers, but Mom wouldn't be home from work for another hour. She felt her heart begin to pound as panic seeped into her belly.

Suddenly she heard the voice of Amy, her friend who lived across the street. "Hey, mister," Amy's voice called, "you need something? We watch out for each other around here."

Then the deep voice of Amy's seventeen-year-old brother added, "Can I call someone for you? The police are just a dial tone away."

The pounding immediately stopped. A voice answered, "Uh. . .no. I had some business with the man of the house. I'll try again later."

Rachel peeked out the living room curtain to see the man quickly retreating down the sidewalk as Amy and her brother stood on their front porch, watching.

"Thank you so much for coming to my rescue," Rachel said as she hugged Amy.

"That's what friends *do*—I've got your back, and you've got mine!"

Whisper of Wisdom

*There is a friend who sticks
closer than a brother.*
Proverbs 18:24 AMP

Fruits of the Spirit

*There are certain ways to identify a Christian.
We need to take a look at ourselves and make sure
that we are being true representatives of Christ.*

What do your friends have to say about you? Would they be surprised if they learned that you are a Christian? The mark of a true Christian is that Jesus can be seen in every area of her life. There are certain traits that help identify a child of God. Love, joy, patience, and kindness are just a few. Do you believe that your friends would know by your love of others, your patience, and your kindness that you are a follower of Christ?

Take a look at your actions and your attitudes and make sure they line up with the fruits of a true Christian. Jesus asks His children to be like Him in the way they deal with others. In fact, it's our treatment of others that sets us apart in the world. Jesus modeled perfect sacrifice and love for others. We need to share that love with those around us.

Whisper of Wisdom

The fruit of the Spirit is love, joy, peace, patience, kindness, goodness, faithfulness, gentleness and self-control. Against such things there is no law.

GALATIANS 5:22–23 NIV

A Princess White

Can you judge your work at first glance?
That second look may put things in a different light.

Find an old pair of your white socks. Do they look white to you? Now grab a pair of new white socks. Suddenly you're unsure if the older pair is white after all. So when God gives you a specific job to do, how do you know if what you do hits or misses the "white" mark?

Say that God nudges you to invite a not-so-well-liked classmate to your house for supper. Your moms agree she can come. Well, if you compare what you did to doing nothing at all, you may think you did great. Ask a good friend and she'll pat you on the back. The real test comes when you hold your work up to the purity of God's Word. Does it still look "white"?

The assignment that you kind of dreaded ends up being a great time—for both you and your classmate. When God helps His princess pass the "white" test, you have something to shout about!

Whisper of Wisdom

We won't brag about something we don't have a
right to brag about. We will only brag about the work
that God has sent us to do, and you are part of that work.

2 Corinthians 10:13 cev

Please Don't Tell!

The Bible tells us that someone who is trustworthy can keep a confidence. But are you expected to keep all secrets?

How many times have you been told, "I have something to tell you, but you *can't* tell *anyone*!" Often that begins a discussion about gossip, a "special someone," or some other top-secret information. But what if a friend confessed, "I'm taking drugs"? Is that a secret you should keep?

When a friend is harming herself or being harmed, she needs help, and as much as you would like to give that help, you can't tackle something that big alone. Tell her that you'd like to go with her so that she can get the help she needs. She may feel comfortable with a pastor, a teacher, or even your parent.

God gave us friends not only to have fun with but also to help out when things get tough. Just as you need help from others at times, they need help from you. Offer to lend a hand, and with strength from God, you can be part of the plan to get your friend the help she needs.

Whisper of Wisdom

*To him who is about to faint and despair,
kindness is due from his friend.*

JOB 6:14 AMP

Hide-and-Seek

Hide-and-seek is a fun game to play, but we never have to worry about God hiding from us. He's always near!

Isn't it fun to play hide-and-seek in the dark with a bunch of your friends? But it's not so much fun when you've searched for fifteen minutes and can't find anyone. Then it gets a little annoying and sometimes even scary—especially in the dark. That's when you want to yell, "Olly, olly, oxen free!" and let all of your friends come running out of their hiding spots.

We never have to ask God to come out of His hiding place. He is always near when we call on Him. James 4:8 tells us that if we come near to God, He will come near to us! Isn't that wonderful? We don't have to go searching for God in the dark, wondering where He's hiding. Just come near to Him—pray to Him and read His Word—and He will come near to you!

Whisper of Wisdom

[God] doesn't play hide-and-seek with us. He's not remote; he's near. We live and move in him, can't get away from him!
ACTS 17:27–28 MSG

Wildfire

Gossip may start out fun, but it soon gets out of control.
God wants you to stop gossip in its tracks.

*H*ave you ever heard a juicy piece of information about someone else that you just couldn't keep to yourself? God calls this sharing of news gossip. And He *hates* it.

God hates gossip because it devastates relationships, ruins reputations, and shatters self-confidence. It's the spark that can ignite an angry fire among friends, and once it starts, it's hard to stop.

So what should you do if you're stuck in a line of gossipers, learning the latest and greatest embarrassment of so-and-so? Smother the flames by changing the subject. If that doesn't work, explain that you'd rather not hear about the news and that the person being talked about probably doesn't want everyone to know.

Gossip—especially gossip among friends—is often very difficult to stop. But like a wildfire, the hurtful cycle can be stopped with enough persistence. Ask God to make you aware of the gossip fires in your life so that you can work toward extinguishing them.

Whisper of Wisdom

When you run out of wood, the fire goes out;
when the gossip ends, the quarrel dies down.
PROVERBS 26:20 MSG

God Will Forgive You—Always!

If you ever find yourself doubting God's love for you, remember this: His love is so perfect that when you tell Him you're sorry, He'll wrap His arms around you and whisper, "I forgive you."

Have you ever messed up big-time and thought, *Uh-oh, now I've done it. I feel so bad about what I've done. I wonder if God will ever forgive me.*

Maybe you told a lie. Maybe you cheated on a test at school. Maybe you were mean to your friend and made her cry.

While all of us will occasionally make mistakes and fail to be "perfect," it's a comfort to know that God has promised in His Word to forgive us—*no matter what*. He loves each of us so much that there's nothing we could do to cause Him to turn His back on us—no matter how big or bad our sin may seem.

Need forgiveness from God? Simply ask, and you'll have it!

Whisper of Wisdom

"Come now, let's settle this," says the LORD. "Though your sins are like scarlet, I will make them as white as snow. Though they are red like crimson, I will make them as white as wool."

ISAIAH 1:18 NLT

Break Away!

Find a secret place—a quiet place—and pray.

Imagine you're at a party and lots of people are there. You see an old friend, someone you hardly ever get to talk to. You go outside, away from the noise and confusion, so that you can spend some time together. Isn't it wonderful to visit—just the two of you? It's the same in your relationship with God. He longs to spend time with you.

Whether you're with your friends, your family, or the people from your church, life can get really loud and crazy! It's exciting to hang out with lots of people and have a great time, but it's also wonderful to sneak away for some quiet time with your heavenly Father. He doesn't just want you to talk to Him; He wants you to listen. It's easier to hear His voice when you're quiet and still, which is why it's important to get away from the crowd.

In the secret place, you're telling God that you love just hanging out with Him. Every princess should tell her Daddy-God that she adores Him. So break away from the crowd today—and do just that!

Whisper of Wisdom

Jesus often withdrew to lonely places and prayed.
LUKE 5:16 NIV

Ghosts of the Past

No way out. No escape.

Memories are a precious thing. . .unless you're being haunted by bad, painful ones that you can't stop thinking about, no matter how hard you try. Like the time you broke something valuable, or lost someone you loved. Maybe something awful happened to you and the memory of that experience chases you like a specter in the night.

Tragedies come when you least expect them, and the effects of those events can trouble you for a long time. The key to overcoming is letting go and moving on. You can't change the past. The broken valuable and lost loved one are gone forever, and no amount of wishing will bring them back. Your bad memories are just that. Memories. And there comes a time when you have to let them go.

It sounds easy, but you know it isn't, and God knows that, too. He understands how much you're hurting and is ready to help you overcome. With His help, you can banish the ghosts of your past and reach forward to the bright future just waiting to be discovered.

Whisper of Wisdom

But this one thing I do, forgetting those things which are behind, and reaching forth unto those things which are before.

PHILIPPIANS 3:13 KJV

Honestly!

C'mon, you can do it!
Speak truth in every situation—even the hard ones!

Do you promise to tell the whole truth and nothing but the truth. . .in every situation? Might sound impossible, but that's what God expects from His girls.

Imagine this—your best friend is sitting next to you in class and she looks over at your test, wanting to copy the answers. You're embarrassed and scared, especially when the teacher notices and asks you what happened. It would be easier to tell a little white lie than confess the truth—especially since you know your best friend will be mad at you for telling on her! Surely you can get away with a "little" lie. . .just this once.

Wrong! The problem with little white lies is there's nothing little about them! They're huge in God's sight. More important, He sees all the way down to the heart. That means God knows when we're being dishonest, even if no one else does—and it breaks His heart.

A daughter of the King is a truth-teller! Dare to be different—especially in the tough times!

Whisper of Wisdom

Truthful lips endure forever,
but a lying tongue lasts only a moment.
PROVERBS 12:19 NIV

A Comfort

When we know others are hurting, we should try to help them.

In this life, we all experience some hard times. But with God's help and comfort, we get through them and come out on the other side, stronger and wiser. Then when a friend goes through the same sort of situation, we remember how we felt; we know what comforted us.

When one of your friends is having a hard time, try to remember the times you have had that were hard for you. Maybe someone in her family is sick or has passed away. Your friend might have just failed a test or gotten a bad report card. Or maybe her feelings have been hurt by someone. Or maybe she just had a fight with someone. If any of those things has happened to you, try to remember how you felt. What made you feel better? Perhaps it was a card you got in the mail, saying how much the sender loved you. Perhaps it was just a nice hug from a Sunday school teacher. Maybe it was something as simple as an understanding smile from your mom, or a friend letting you know she was praying for you.

Whatever made you feel better, whatever comfort you once received, try giving that same comfort to your friend. God gives us comfort through our troubles, and He wants us to comfort others when they are hurting.

Whisper of Wisdom

Praise be to the God and Father of our Lord Jesus Christ, the Father of compassion and the God of all comfort, who comforts us in all our troubles, so that we can comfort those in any trouble with the comfort we ourselves have received from God.

2 Corinthians 1:3–4 niv

Work for the Lord

*There is much to be done, and your part is important.
Stay with it to the end.*

God designed you in a special way, and He planned a special job just for you. He could have chosen any other way to accomplish the task, but He chose to get it done through you. What an awesome privilege to be able to do something for God!

Not everyone has the same job to do. Sometimes it might not be easy to know exactly what God is telling you to do, but when you read the Bible, pray, and listen to the Holy Spirit, God's way becomes clear. If you do the things every Christian should do, God will plainly show you the specific job He has for you. Be faithful to tell your friends and family about God's love. Some will listen; some will not—but God will honor your obedience and will bless your faithfulness.

Whisper of Wisdom

*Be ye stedfast, unmoveable, always abounding
in the work of the Lord, forasmuch as ye know
that your labour is not in vain in the Lord.*

1 CORINTHIANS 15:58 KJV

What about Me?

Do you ever get tired of doing nice things for other people? What about me? you may be thinking. When is something wonderful going to happen for me? Just continue being kind, and see what's in store for you!

You volunteer your free time at the local animal shelter. You donate new and used books, clothes, and toys to charity every year. And you regularly visit the retirement home and play games with lonely residents. That's in addition to the little unremembered acts of kindness you do throughout the rest of the year. And to be honest, you're getting a little worn out from all this "doing good" stuff. You even find yourself wondering if it's worth all the effort.

If we focus on others instead of ourselves, we'll begin to see the effect of our good deeds. And God will have a hand in that. He sees what we're doing to make a difference in the lives of others, and He promises that we will experience something good because of it. While people may overlook or forget our kindnesses, isn't it wonderful to know that God never will? Today, ask the Lord to give you the strength and energy you need to keep up the good work. And then wait and see what good things He brings your way!

Whisper of Wisdom

Let us not become weary in doing good, for at the proper time we will reap a harvest if we do not give up.

GALATIANS 6:9 NIV

A Simple Rule

Being nice isn't always easy.
But God will help you show His love if you just ask.

Mia had a two-word reminder taped up in her locker that she looked at every time she opened the door: BE NICE.

"That seems like a good rule to follow," her friend Justin observed as the two opened their lockers to switch books between classes. "But why do you have to remind yourself to be nice?"

"Because I don't always *want* to be nice," Mia said. "But these two words remind me to ask Jesus to help me follow His commandment when He said, 'Do to others whatever you would like them to do to you.' When I pray, I know He shows me ways to demonstrate His love to others."

Some people mistakenly think Jesus commanded the Golden Rule so that if we do good things for others, they'll do good things back. While some people will return good for good, others will return evil for good. Instead, Jesus' simple instruction encourages Christians to show others grace that may lead others to their own faith someday.

Whisper of Wisdom

"Do to others whatever you would like them to do to you."
MATTHEW 7:12 NLT

The Beat Goes On

God uses our weaknesses to show His strength.

Andi wanted it so badly, she felt like she'd burst. But she was almost afraid to hope; her hopes had been dashed too many times before.

Life had never been easy. Andi was born with cerebral palsy, a muscular disorder that caused her to have to wear leg braces since she learned to walk, and to have uncoordinated hands that made handling objects very difficult.

But music had been her very heartbeat. As far back as she could remember, she'd tapped out the rhythm to every song on the radio. She even took drum lessons despite her doctor's opinion that she would never be able to hold drumsticks or move her limbs quickly enough to keep up with a fast tempo.

And now, Andi was nervously waiting for the results of her tryout for the church youth praise band. She'd done her best and could sense God's power helping her.

"Lord," she whispered, "I can do nothing without You. But You can do *everything*. And You are my strength. I leave the results up to You."

As Andi finished her prayer, she looked up to see the youth director headed her way with a huge smile on his face.

Whisper of Wisdom

When I am weak, then I am strong.
2 CORINTHIANS 12:10 NLT

Step It Up!

Did you know that God loves it when you give your very best?

*H*e does! The Bible says that God wants His girls to concentrate on doing their best for Him. He loves it when you "step it up." If you're looking for some great ways to do that, here are some suggestions: Give God your very best attitude (even when it's really hard). Give Him your best time of day. (Don't wait until you're too tired to pray and read your Bible.) Give an offering at church. (Putting money in the offering plate is a great way to show that you're dedicated to Him.)

There are dozens of other ways you can step it up! For example, you could collect canned goods to donate to your church's food pantry. Make a game of it. (Everyone loves a challenge!) Or maybe you could donate clothing or blankets for the homeless in the wintertime.

Oh, there are a zillion ways to help out! And a daughter of the King loves to give—of her time, talents, and treasures. She gives her Father her very best, so step it up, princess!

Whisper of Wisdom

Concentrate on doing your best for God, work you won't be ashamed of, laying out the truth plain and simple.
2 TIMOTHY 2:15 MSG

Best of Friends

Friendships may come unglued like a postage stamp from an envelope. Will you be a friend who sticks close?

It's easy to hang out with a friend when things are *up*, but how do you treat her when somebody else puts her *down*? God reminds His princess that a friend loves at all times, and He gives you a great example from the Old Testament.

Jonathan and David were best buddies, but Jonathan's father, King Saul, tried his best to put David down. King Saul was angry and envied young David because he was turning out to be a better soldier than the king. Instead of going along with Saul's plan to harm David, Jonathan hung in there with his best friend. He gave his father rave reviews of how David had risked his life in battle.

Most of all, Jonathan encouraged Saul to come close to their heavenly Father. It's great to stick close to your friend, but the greatest thing is that you both stick close to God.

Whisper of Wisdom

Jonathan spoke with his father about David,
saying many good things about him.
1 Samuel 19:4 nlt

How Big Is God?

Is there a Goliath in your life?
Don't ever forget that God is bigger!

Remember the story of David and Goliath? It's in the Old Testament in 1 Samuel 17. A shepherd boy named David faced a huge giant named Goliath who was a Philistine. Goliath was a grown man over nine feet tall, and everybody in the land that David lived in was terrified of this giant. But David remembered that God is bigger than anything and anyone and that He was always with him.

God had kept David safe from lions and bears while he was watching the sheep. David said, "The Lord who delivered me from the paw of the lion and the paw of the bear will deliver me from the hand of this Philistine" (1 Samuel 17:37 NIV). David defeated the giant with only a stone and a sling because the power of God was with him.

Do you know that God's power is with you, too? Is there something in your life right now that just seems way too big to handle by yourself? Remember that God is bigger, and just as He was with David, He will be with you!

Whisper of Wisdom

What, then, shall we say in response to this?
If God is for us, who can be against us?
ROMANS 8:31 NIV

Words, Words, Words

Bad words are like poison; they take other people down.
God wants you to be an encouragement instead.

Bullies are people who tear others down to make themselves feel better. They're mean and rude and not fun to be around.

Everyone has moments of bully-ness. "Hey, Sarah, nice haircut. Did your dad do it with his hedge trimmers?" "Did you see what Rachel's wearing today? Did she get dressed in the dark?"

God hates mean words like these—even if we use them in small doses. Mean words can leave lasting wounds. They can damage people's self-esteem and cause them to be mean to other people.

God's will for His children is that every word that comes out of our lips is helpful and builds others up. That doesn't mean we have to be fake about our words. God wants sincere encouragement to be on our lips. Ask God to give you a spirit of goodness that spills over into your daily conversation. You never know when a kind word will brighten someone else's day.

Whisper of Wisdom

Don't use foul or abusive language. Let everything you say be good and helpful, so that your words will be an encouragement to those who hear them.

Ephesians 4:29 NLT

Mirror, Mirror, on the Wall

Who is the fairest in God's kingdom?
Those who have a beautiful spirit.

Have you ever scowled at your reflection in the mirror? Maybe your ears are too big and your hair is a wild, curly mess. Maybe your smile is crooked and your nose is covered with freckles. But have you ever stopped to think of how beautiful you are on the inside?

The qualities that you possess as God's child are more dazzling than dimples.

Your sweetness and honesty, the joy that you shower on others. . .all of these things make you beautiful! Never mind that you're too short or too tall. When it comes to spiritual good looks, you're a knockout! So the next time you look in the mirror, don't worry about the color of your eyes. Instead, imagine what your heavenly Father says to all the angels in heaven when He sees the *real* you—the part deep down inside.

"There's My daughter—isn't she lovely?"

Whisper of Wisdom

Blessed are the pure in heart:
for they shall see God.
MATTHEW 5:8 KJV

What Season Is It?

*Winter, spring, summer, fall. . .
Can I really trust God
through it all?*

The Bible tells us that everything has its season. Maybe you've been waiting for something to happen, but it's just not the right season yet. Hang on, princess! Your day is coming!

Imagine you're in a "springtime" season. Everything in your life is blooming. You have great new friendships, you're growing in the Lord—basically everything is going well. Then summer comes.

Everything is now sunny and in full bloom. You're in a great relationship with your parents and getting along well with your brothers and sisters.

Next comes fall. Maybe you notice that some of your friendships are coming to an end, or perhaps there are other changes in your life. Maybe you used to take dance lessons and now you don't; or maybe you were on a ball team and now you're not. Things are winding down. After fall comes winter. If you're in a winter season, maybe nothing seems to be working out. Perhaps you're lonely or disconnected—having a hard time with your prayer life.

No matter what season you're in, remember: That season will come to an end, and another will soon begin.

Whisper of Wisdom

*There is a time for everything,
and a season for every activity under heaven.*

ECCLESIASTES 3:1 NIV

Just Believe

We believe in the Lord, even though we cannot see Him.

You know you are God's princess, and you want to have a home in heaven with Him one day. Even though you cannot see Him right now, one day you will—as long as you believe in Him.

The Bible tells us that after Jesus died and was resurrected, He appeared to all the disciples except for Thomas. When the others who had seen the resurrected Jesus told Thomas about it, Thomas did not believe them. In fact, he told his friends, "Unless I see the nail holes in his hands, put my finger in the nail holes, and stick my hand in his side, I won't believe it" (John 20:25 MSG).

Eight days later Jesus showed up again, this time when Thomas was around. With Jesus standing right in front of him, Thomas now had no doubt that He had indeed come back from the dead! What was Jesus' response? "So, you believe because you've seen with your own eyes. Even better blessings are in store for those who believe without seeing" (John 20:29 MSG).

You know what, princess? You have many blessings in store because you believe in Jesus without seeing Him. What a way to live!

Whisper of Wisdom

We live by what we believe,
not by what we can see.

2 CORINTHIANS 5:7 NCV

An Acquired Taste

Eating good food helps us stay healthy. The same is true for our spiritual health. When you regularly feed your soul the best food available—God's Word—you become a stronger, healthier Christian.

Most people don't start out liking vegetables even though they are valuable and healthy foods. It takes time and exposure to develop a taste for the foods that are good for you.

What are you feeding your soul? Are you filling your heart and mind with the world's music, cartoons, and television programs? If so, retrain your appetite by spending more time reading God's Word, listening to Christian music, and reading good books.

You may not always feel like obeying God's Word, attending church, or taking part in wholesome activities, but doing those things over and over helps to develop your appetite for them. Jesus tells us that if we come to Him, He will fill us with spiritual food so that we will never be hungry. So even though you may not always feel like learning more about God or doing the things you know you should, do them anyway. He will bless you for your faithfulness, and you may be surprised at how your appetite changes.

Whisper of Wisdom

Then Jesus said, "I am the bread that gives life.
Whoever comes to me will never be hungry,
and whoever believes in me will never be thirsty."

JOHN 6:35 NCV

Eternal Reward

Don't be afraid to witness. Be willing to take a stand.
The eternal result is worth it.

Savannah stared at the homework assignment with concern. She had to write an essay entitled "What I Believe." It could be about any topic as long as it was a belief she was defending.

Savannah knew what she must do. She had to take this opportunity to take a stand for Jesus. She realized that because her teacher was not a Christian, he might give her a low grade. She remembered something her Sunday school teacher had said recently.

"You might be ridiculed or rejected if you take a stand for Jesus, but that only lasts a little while. The reward you receive for being faithful to God will be eternal. It's sure worth it!"

Savannah would write that essay! She'd do her very best, and whatever grade she received, she would accept. Then she'd look forward to her eternal reward.

Whisper of Wisdom

Our light affliction, which is but for a moment,
worketh for us a far more exceeding
and eternal weight of glory.
2 Corinthians 4:17 KJV

Which Way from Here?

If you like to see the sun rise, which direction do you need to look? Looking in the wrong direction may cause you to miss it.

If you're bike riding with some other kids, and a few "brave" ones start going into "No Trespassing" territory, that's the time for God's princess to head in another direction. Saying no to trouble isn't popular, but that response makes a big hit with God.

So what kind of unsafe places does Solomon warn you about? In the verses surrounding today's Bible verse, he urges you to refuse an invitation to gain something for yourself by harming other people's property, privacy, or personal dignity. God will help you to rearrange your steps so you can take off in another direction. Do it as quickly as you would take your finger off a hot stove.

God wants to keep His princess from getting burned, so ask Him to give you a good sense of direction. He can keep you heading the right way instead of venturing into trouble. Why look in the wrong direction?

Whisper of Wisdom

My child, if sinners entice you,
turn your back on them!
PROVERBS 1:10 NLT

Construction, Not Demolition

*An encouraging word makes the other person feel good.
And it'll make you feel good, too.*

Little kids love to build a tower of blocks or sculpt a sand castle only to gleefully stomp it to the ground. Destruction seems to be an instinct for humans.

God knows that our sinful nature gets pleasure out of seeing other people stomped to the ground. Even when we know what it's like to be on the receiving end of insults and mean words, sometimes we take pleasure in adding to the destruction of others by piling on words that are hurtful and mean spirited.

Our heavenly Father doesn't want to see His children destroy one another with words. His plan is encouragement. With every sincere, kind word, God adds another building block to the life of His child. And with every block of encouragement, we are made stronger to stand up to any destructive, stomping words that come our way.

Spend time today adding building blocks of encouragement to people around you. Soon you'll see that you'll be made stronger, too.

Whisper of Wisdom

*Encourage each other and build each other up,
just as you are already doing.*

1 THESSALONIANS 5:11 NLT

Sugar and Spice

Doing good doesn't always pay off in this world.
Thankfully, it is a heavenly reward that we seek.

People have mixed-up motives sometimes. You'll probably even be wrongly accused of something now and then. Sometimes it happens so that the accuser can avoid trouble, but other times it will happen simply because the world can't stand the influence of Christ and wants to get in the way of it whenever it can. The kindness and goodness of a follower of Christ are like salt in a wound to an unbeliever.

Thankfully, we are not accountable to other people for our actions. We are only accountable to God, who sees what is done and understands the motives of the heart. So no matter what people say about your actions, if your motives are pure and you are doing right before God, you have nothing to worry about. Jesus was wrongly accused, but He knew that His Father knew the truth, so He didn't even try to defend Himself. Try to live with such confidence that it just doesn't matter what other people say; it only matters what Jesus says.

Whisper of Wisdom

Always let others see you behaving properly,
even though they may still accuse you of doing
wrong. Then on the day of judgment, they will honor
God by telling the good things they saw you do.

1 PETER 2:12 CEV

Remember Me

What do you want others to know you for?
How does God want you to be remembered?

It's not that you were the quiz team champion, but that you helped your little brother with math. It's not that you made the cheerleading squad, but that you encouraged the girl with speech problems.

It's the little things we do as Christians to help other children of God that will be remembered after this school year, after you graduate from school, even after you die. These are the things God will recall when you finally meet Him face-to-face.

So the next time you are tempted to go for selfish glory, think how God gets the most glory from the small acts of kindness and service that we do for others.

Whisper of Wisdom

"Then those 'sheep' are going to say, 'Master, what are you talking about? When did we ever see you hungry and feed you, thirsty and give you a drink? And when did we ever see you sick or in prison and come to you?' Then the King will say, 'I'm telling the solemn truth: Whenever you did one of these things to someone overlooked or ignored, that was me—you did it to me.' "
MATTHEW 25:37-40 MSG

Give It Up!

*Loosen those fingers!
Let it go, princess.*

Imagine you're holding something in your hand. Your fingers are wrapped tightly around it. You don't want to let go, no matter how many times you're told you should. So you keep it clutched in your fist.

Begin to loosen your grip, princess! Release those fingers. . .one at a time. Now take a close look. What's inside? What have you been holding on to?

Worries? You've been hanging on to your worries and cares? Well, it's time to let them go. Give them to the Lord! His hands are much bigger than yours, after all—and He wants to hold them for you.

Wave your hands up in the air. Feel those burdens lifting? Can you see your worries flying away? You were never meant to hold on to them in the first place, you know. God wants His daughters to live a worry-free life. So the next time you're tempted to worry, remember to open up those hands and let your troubles fly far, far away—straight to the heart of your Father.

Whisper of Wisdom

*Give all your worries and cares to God,
for he cares about you.*

1 PETER 5:7 NLT

Christ in You

You are alive in Christ. He lives in you.
You live by faith in Him.

You know that when you asked Jesus to be your Savior, you received new life, but have you ever really stopped to think about what that means? First of all, recognizing that you are a sinner and accepting God's gift of salvation is the best decision you ever made, but it doesn't stop there. You are no longer a slave to your sinful nature. You've been set free. You're a new creature.

Think about nature in springtime. You see a nest full of eggs. It doesn't look like much, but you know that inside those eggs, new little creatures are waiting to hatch and begin life. When they finally do hatch, they're still helpless and awkward, but oh, the potential that's there! When you first trusted Jesus, you were like that little bird—a new creature. You had a ways to go in your spiritual walk, but with Jesus you could realize the full potential of your new life.

Whisper of Wisdom

I am crucified with Christ: nevertheless I live; yet not I,
but Christ liveth in me: and the life which I now
live in the flesh I live by the faith of the Son of God,
who loved me, and gave himself for me.

GALATIANS 2:20 KJV

A Promise for Honoring Your Parents

When you love and respect your parents, you'll be blessed.

God has given us commandments to live by, and He has given us promises to look forward to, too. The first commandment He gave us has a wonderful promise that goes with it. That commandment is to honor your father and mother. That means to treat them with great respect and to obey them.

Your parents love you and want only the best for you. And the best is to be a child of God, His princess through and through.

Your parents have a big responsibility—to teach you about God and how to walk with Him. And if you honor them as God says to do, He promises that you will live a long life full of blessing.

Wow, a princess with lots of blessings, including loving parents and a loving God! It doesn't get any better than that!

Whisper of Wisdom

*Respect your father and mother. This is the first
Law given that had a promise. The promise is this:
If you respect your father and mother, you will live a
long time and your life will be full of many good things.*
EPHESIANS 6:2-3 NLV

Happiness That Lasts!

What makes you happy? Getting stuff you want?
Spending time with your friends? Or is it something more?

Your friend just got a new iPod, and you can't help but feel a little envious. After all, you've been wanting an iPod for as long as you can remember. . .and you're still waiting. To make matters worse, you're the only one in your group of friends who doesn't have one, and it doesn't look like you'll have one anytime soon.

The more you hear about your friend's new "treasure," the harder it is for you to be even a little happy for her. *Why should she get everything she wants?* you think. *I deserve stuff I want, too!*

It's so easy to fall into the "I want" trap. But once you get that longed-for item, will you really be satisfied? Maybe for just a little while, but eventually you will have an itch for something new.

In God's Word, He reminds us that earthly things won't ever make us truly happy. Only when we focus on things eternal—like our relationship with Jesus Christ—will we find happiness that lasts for a lifetime.

Whisper of Wisdom

"Watch yourselves! Keep from wanting all kinds of things you should not have. A man's life is not made up of things, even if he has many riches."
LUKE 12:15 NLV

Just Doing Your
Princess Thing

Do you tell your eyes to blink or your stomach to growl?
Some things come naturally.

You may not think about the fact that while you're busy going here and there all day, your heart beats continually. Each day it does its thing for you, whether it's a sunny weekend or a dreary morning. That's what kind of a friend God wants you to be—one who hangs in there with a buddy, no matter whether the sun is shining or dark clouds are forming.

A "heartbeat" princess shows up for the fun times and crummy times, too. Misunderstandings, disagreements, or mood changes can actually strengthen your friendship, just as vigorous exercise lifts the heart to a new level of good health. A "heartbeat" friend also expresses love quietly, just as your heart doesn't announce to everyone what it's doing. It simply does it. Without fanfare, your loving words and actions help your friend to keep going strong.

Will you take God up on His invitation to be a princess with a friendly "heartbeat"? Your friend may not think about your consistent "heartbeat"; neither does she know what she'd do without it.

Whisper of Wisdom

A friend loves at all times.

PROVERBS 17:17 NIV

God-Confidence

Do you have self-confidence or God-confidence?
Let's find out which is better. . . .

*A*re your friends always telling you that you should have more confidence? Or maybe you have a *ton* of confidence and you are proud of it! Well, the Bible says that self-confidence is useless! Can you believe that? Our confidence should be based only on our relationship with God.

Philippians 4:13 tells us that we can do all things through Christ who give us strength. So if you're one of those girls who doesn't have a lot of confidence, ask God to give you His confidence. You can do all things through Christ! The next time you have to get up in class and read a book report or do anything else that brings you center stage, remember that although self-confidence is useless, God-confidence is all-strengthening and only a prayer away! But if you happen to be one of those girls with a ton of self-confidence, ask God to help you focus more on Him. That way whenever you have to do something in public, the focus will be on God instead of on you. God-confidence is so much better!

Whisper of Wisdom

Forget about self-confidence; it's useless.
Cultivate God-confidence.
1 Corinthians 10:12 msg

Bite Your Tongue

Your tongue is a powerful tool.
Use it for good instead of evil.

Your tongue is made up of sixteen muscles that help you create sounds, syllables, and the thousands of words that you say every day. The tongue can be your greatest friend or your worst enemy, depending on what words you choose to form with it.

The Bible compares the tongue to an animal that's so wild and dangerous, it's impossible to tame. "People can tame all kinds of animals, birds, reptiles, and fish, but no one can tame the tongue. It is restless and evil, full of deadly poison" (James 3:7-8 NLT).

If you have the right attitude, your tongue can proclaim the message of Christ by building others up with kind words and sincere praise to God. If you have the wrong attitude, your tongue can produce rudeness, deceit, and even devastation.

God tells us to keep our tongues from evil and lies. Keeping our tongues from these sins may mean shutting our mouths and letting the sixteen tongue muscles rest. Spend time today asking God to show you when to speak and when to simply bite your tongue.

Whisper of Wisdom

Keep your tongue from evil and your lips from speaking lies.
PSALM 34:13 NIV

The Cure for "I Need More"

Paul learned how to be content.
We can, too! It's all in how you look at it.

In a world full of all kinds of "stuff," it's easy to get caught up in thinking that we need something, when in fact, it really should go in the "want" category. Think of something you need. Is it really a need? Or would it be considered more of a want?

Our basic needs are food, clothing, and shelter. The wants are the "extras" that go beyond that—eating out, that cute new outfit, or a bedroom makeover. There isn't anything wrong with these wants in themselves, but it's easy to cross the line to discontentment when we don't get them.

Thank God today for what He has given you. And while you're in that attitude of thanks, why not tell your parents that you appreciate how they take care of your needs?

Let's take a lesson from Paul, who said that he wouldn't complain; rather, he would be satisfied with what he had.

Whisper of Wisdom

I am not complaining about having too little.
I have learned to be satisfied with whatever I have.

Philippians 4:11 CEV

A Princess Pop-up

Looking for something to perk up your friendships?
Does Paul have an idea for you!

As soon as your phone rings, you jump up to answer it, right? When you see a letter addressed to you, automatically you tear into it. Just like most people, you respond that way naturally. So what kind of reaction does God want you, His princess, to have the second one of your friends pops into your mind?

The apostle Paul said that as soon as he called his friends to mind, he sent up a prayer to thank God for them. Hey, princess, why not jump right into a prayer of thanks as soon as a friend's face flits across your mind? Take a minute to thank God for bringing her into your life. Naturally you'll want to thank God for the ways she's cared about you. The best reason of all to pray for her, Paul might say, is that once you think of her, you just can't help saying, "Thanks, God!"

Like jumping up to answer the phone, spring into action the second a friend pops into your mind. You'll both be blessed when you pop right into a prayer of thanks.

Whisper of Wisdom

Every time I think of you,
I give thanks to my God.
PHILIPPIANS 1:3 NLT

Tough Stuff

Let the weak say, "I am strong!"

*D*o you ever feel like Popeye—before he eats his spinach? Feel worn out and tired? Need an extra dose of strength and courage?

We all go through times when our faith is low, when we don't feel like we have the energy to pray for the big stuff. The tough stuff. But here's the cool thing about God—even when we are at our weakest, He is still strong. (Aren't you glad God never gets tired?) He wants you to lean on Him when you're weak, to draw from His strength.

Let's say you have a big prayer need—a huge one. Maybe someone in your family is really sick, or your parents are going through a crisis. Maybe you've prayed and prayed, and nothing seems to be happening. Even if you feel like your strength is gone, remember that God hasn't changed. He's still right there—on the throne—and He will strengthen you if you ask Him to. So ask! Approach the throne of your Daddy-God and ask Him for courage to get you through the storms you're facing.

Whisper of Wisdom

As soon as I pray, you answer me;
you encourage me by giving me strength.

PSALM 138:3 NLT

God Is Love

*Love is of God, so a person who is
in Christ cannot be filled with hate.*

*O*il and water simply do not mix. You can stir them together and try to get them to blend, but they will not join. The same is true with hate and love. They are two emotions that cannot exist together. It is impossible for someone to profess to know God but live with hate and bitterness toward others.

Jesus says that loves comes from Him. So if we truly know Him, then we allow Him to change our hearts. It is impossible for a heart changed by God to remain filled with hate and anger. If you know someone like that, someone who struggles with bitterness or a bad temper, pray that the love of Jesus will fill his or her heart so that there is no longer room for those things. If you struggle with bad feelings or hate toward someone, you need to ask God to forgive those feelings and to wash them clean from your heart. He will replace the hate that you feel with His love.

Whisper of Wisdom

*Dear friends, let us love one another, for love comes from God.
Everyone who loves has been born of God and knows God.
Whoever does not love does not know God, because God is love.*

1 John 4:7-8 niv

The Princess Choice

How would you feel? The $20 bill you want to deposit, the banker tells you, is a counterfeit.

Among your collection of prized dolls, you think you know which one is worth a lot, until someone who knows "doll stuff" tells you differently. So what if someone into "God stuff" informed you that the one you worship has no value, either?

When Paul, the traveling missionary, visited the people in Athens in the first century, he saw a collection of shrines for their many gods, but they didn't know the true God, even His name. Paul courageously pointed out that the one God they didn't value very highly was worth everything. In fact, He created everything! What about their gods? They were counterfeit, not gods at all.

God will give His princess the courage to point others to the God who is worthy of their worship. How sad if they bank on counterfeit gods!

Whisper of Wisdom

"Now what you worship as something unknown I am going to proclaim to you."

ACTS 17:23 NIV

From Invisible. . .to Visible!

Can we really believe in a God we can't see?
You bet we can!

Isn't it interesting to think that God created the heavens and the earth just by speaking them into existence? He's pretty good at making something. . .out of nothing. Talk about amazing! And the very things He created—the rocks, rivers, trees, and so forth—sing His praises! Best of all, He created all of those things for us!

What about you? What if you were asked to make a cake. . .but were given no ingredients? No flour. No eggs. No oil. Nothing. Could you do it? Could you speak the word *cake* and expect one to miraculously appear? Of course not! Only God can perform miracles. And though we can't see Him, we know that He is there, working them every day in our lives.

It takes a lot of faith to believe in a God we can't see, but when we look around at this beautiful planet (which He created for our enjoyment), it's easy to tell He's an awesome, miracle-working God! Praise Him, princess!

Whisper of Wisdom

By faith we understand that the universe
was formed at God's command, so that what
is seen was not made out of what was visible.

HEBREWS 11:3 NIV

All God's Children

You're a child of God. Your friends belong to Him, too.
Your faith makes you sisters in Christ.

So you've always wanted a sister. Did you know you already have one—many, actually? The moment you asked Jesus into your heart, God adopted you into His family. You became His daughter, and you joined all the other girls whom He has adopted.

What a wonderful family to join. God knows just how much you will need your spiritual sisters—big ones and little ones—and He will bring them into your life. Be sure to be paying attention so you know when this happens.

Those "big sisters," ones a little more mature in their faith, can help you get to know God better.

And sometimes you'll be the "big sister," too. God will use you to be an encouragement to another girl. Be willing to obey Him when He asks you to help bring this "little sister" along. It will be one of the best feelings you will ever experience.

Remember: In spite of your differences, you are all God's children. Treat each other with love and kindness, and everyone will be a winner.

Whisper of Wisdom

For ye are all the children of
God by faith in Christ Jesus.
GALATIANS 3:26 KJV

Heavenly Safety

God's promise is that He'll be next to you, no matter how scary the situation.

Shadrach, Meshach, and Abednego knew what real fear is. Their story is told in the book of Daniel, where King Nebuchadnezzar sentenced the three men to death by fire for not bowing down to a gold statue he commanded everyone to worship.

The trio's response to the king's death sentence is pretty amazing: "If we are thrown into the blazing furnace, the God we serve is able to save us from it, and he will rescue us from your hand, O king" (Daniel 3:17 NIV).

That's real faith! These men of God took to heart the promise God makes to His people throughout the Old Testament. God promises to be with us no matter what—through raging waters, blazing fires, wind and storms, car accidents, sickness, family fights, and anything else life can throw our way.

God came through for Shadrach, Meshach, and Abednego in a big way by taking human form and being with the trio in the fire, saving their lives. Your Father in heaven will do no less for you if you have faith that He's always there.

Whisper of Wisdom

"When you pass through the waters, I will be with you; and when you pass through the rivers, they will not sweep over you. When you walk through the fire, you will not be burned; the flames will not set you ablaze."

ISAIAH 43:2 NIV

Who Am I?

Your identity is how you see yourself or how others see you. But how does God identify you, and how does that compare with how you want to be known?

We all have an identity. This means that certain personality traits, and other things that are unique to you, set you apart from other people. If you were asked to describe yourself, what would you say? Would you talk about outward appearance, talents, and other superficial things that are easy to identify, but not really who you are? As believers, we should desire others to see Christ in us and identify us by His presence in our lives.

Unbelievers often try to get Christians to take their eyes off Jesus to focus on worldly things that are used to create worldly identities. They want you to focus on your appearance, your popularity, your talents. But take care to guard yourself from that trap. Know who you are by knowing who He is. Let Jesus' love and His life show you who you are in Him.

Whisper of Wisdom

I've written to warn you about those who are trying to deceive you. But they're no match for what is embedded deeply within you—Christ's anointing. . .[which] teaches you the truth on everything you need to know about yourself and him, uncontaminated by a single lie. Live deeply in what you were taught.

1 JOHN 2:26–27 MSG

Good Thoughts

*When your thoughts are filled with bad things,
push them out of your mind with good thoughts.*

Remember the movie *The Sound of Music*? In it, Julie Andrews, playing a nun-turned-governess, wants to help her charges feel better. So she sings a song called "My Favorite Things." Her idea was to get the kids to think of things that were good rather than of things that were bad—such as the frightening thunderstorm booming all around them.

Have you ever been frightened? Have your worries ever taken over your sense of well-being? Has your mind ever been full of things that you know God does not want you to think about? When that happens, God has a great remedy! Concentrate on His favorite things! Like the truth of Him! Think on what is right. Think pure—clean and wholesome—thoughts. Think on what is lovely—sunsets and sunrises, raindrops on roses, whiskers on kittens, and all the beauty that God has created. Think about all the good people you know and the nice things they do. Think about the things that are worthy of your praise.

If you fill your mind with those good things, all the bad thoughts—your fears, worries, and woes—will disappear. And so will whatever storm clouds have been following you around!

Whisper of Wisdom

*Finally, brothers, whatever is true, whatever is noble,
whatever is right, whatever is pure, whatever is lovely,
whatever is admirable—if anything is excellent or
praiseworthy—think about such things.*

PHILIPPIANS 4:8 NIV

Sticks and Stones

Let's face it: Words hurt!

*Y*ou've probably heard the old saying "Sticks and stones may break my bones, but words will never hurt me." You also know that it's not true. Words *do* hurt. A lot! Being picked on, insulted, and made fun of can be harder to deal with than the ugliest bloody scrape, and can leave a deeper scar.

There's something about a crusty scab that begs to be picked at, and the same is true of injured feelings. It's hard to leave them alone. You want to share them with others, describing the awful things that someone said to you. But the more you relive the offense, the longer it takes to heal.

That's why God wants His children to forgive. It's the only way to cure your wounded feelings. Forgiving means forgetting. It means choosing not to get back at the person who hurt you, even if they did it on purpose.

Jesus was the perfect example of forgiveness. He was slapped, spit on, hated, and put to death on the cross. Yet He forgave His tormentors and asked God to forgive them as well.

The next time someone hurts you, do what Jesus would do. Forgive.

Whisper of Wisdom

For if ye forgive men their trespasses,
your heavenly Father will also forgive you.
MATTHEW 6:14 KJV

The Right Way Out

Feel like you always struggle with the same thing?
Next time you are tempted, look for the right way out!

The Bible tells us that everyone goes through temptation. Everyone sins and struggles with the temptation to do something wrong, so don't feel like you're the only one. The Bible also reminds us that God is faithful and won't ever let us be tempted too much. And you know what? God *promises* that whenever you are tempted to sin, He will *always* provide the right way out! Isn't that cool?

Have you ever looked for the way out before? The next time you're tempted to sin, stop and ask God for the right way out and then look for it! Maybe the phone will ring right when you are tempted to watch a show on TV that isn't a good choice. Or maybe God will help you remember the answer you forgot when you are tempted to cheat on a test. God will surprise you with the right way out—just don't forget to look for it!

Whisper of Wisdom

If you go the wrong way—to the right or to the left—
you will hear a voice behind you saying, "This is
the right way. You should go this way."

ISAIAH 30:21 NCV

The Princess Purr

It's a pleasant sound that isn't heard too often these days.

No, you're not a kitten, but do you know that you can be just as content? If your shoestring breaks in the morning, right before you hurry out the door, you decide to tie a creative knot instead of whining about it. When you come home from school, you spot a new pair of laces in your room. As you pitch the old ones, you're glad you made them work when you had to. Hey, that's a contented sigh God loves to hear from a princess!

Whether you have what you need or not, keep learning to be content in your circumstances. When Paul was in prison, he was running low on stuff but still relaxed contentedly in Christ. After finally receiving a package of goodies, Paul thanked his friends for their gift.

If somebody is slow in coming through for you, God loves to see His princess content with "old shoestrings." He also loves to hear you thank those who help you out of a "knotty" situation.

Whisper of Wisdom

The path of right-living people is level. The Leveler evens the road for the right-living. We're in no hurry, God. We're content to linger in the path sign-posted with your decisions. Who you are and what you've done are all we'll ever want.

Isaiah 26:7–8 MSG

Dream Big

Ballerina, teacher, singer, mother. . .
You can be anything you dream.

What do you most want to do during the life God has given you? Can you see yourself going through training and becoming a skilled performer, trainer, manager, or creator?

Start by praying that your dream comes from God; then begin taking steps to make it happen. The first step for any career is to do your best in school and always be a willing learner in school and out.

Take on an "I can" attitude, like the one found in Philippians 4:13: "I can do all things through Christ who strengthens me" (NKJV). An "I can't" person has lost the game before the national anthem has even played.

And though the look of your dream may change through the years, keep the dream in front of you and keep reaching toward the goal. If God has given you the desire, He will help you become all that you dream of being.

Whisper of Wisdom

We plan the way we want to live,
but only GOD makes us able to live it.
PROVERBS 16:9 MSG

Strong Shoulders

Are there heavy problems you're lugging around?
God's shoulders are strong; He wants to carry them for you.

Makenna's purse was so full of junk that it looked more like a trash bag than a handbag. Most of the stuff she kept inside was old and useless—empty mint tins, gum wrappers, used-up pens, empty lip gloss tubes. More and more junk accumulated in Makenna's purse until it became so heavy that carrying it around made her shoulder ache.

Sometimes in our lives we hold on to worries and stress. Just like the unnecessary junk Makenna kept in her purse, we let troubles and burdens weigh us down until it hurts. God doesn't want you to hold on to your useless problems. He wants to take them from you and carry them on His shoulders so that you can experience true freedom in Christ. Just like Makenna's friend who helped her finally clean out all the junk from her purse, Jesus is ready to take your burdens from you. All you have to do is let Him.

Whisper of Wisdom

Pile your troubles on God's shoulders—he'll carry your load,
he'll help you out. He'll never let good people topple into ruin.
PSALM 55:22 MSG

Costume Jewelry

*The only decoration that Jesus wants us
to focus on is a decoration of the heart.*

Some women spend a lot of time and effort finding big, gaudy pieces
of costume jewelry that cost very little but look very much like the
real thing. They are hoping to make people believe they are wearing
real diamonds or gold. But in reality, the trinkets are just worthless
pieces of plastic. It would be much better if they thought more
about decorating on the inside, dressing up the heart, than about
decorating the outside with junk that will fade away.

Jesus wants girls to be decent and modest. He wants your inner
beauty to be more important to you than your outward appearance.
It matters more to Him how you treat others and how you live for
Him. He doesn't care about your hairstyle, your fancy clothes, or
your makeup. So take your time before rushing into those things. Let
them take a backseat while you work on letting the Holy Spirit grow
you from the inside out.

Whisper of Wisdom

*I also want women to dress modestly,
with decency and propriety, not with braided
hair or gold or pearls or expensive clothes.*
1 TIMOTHY 2:9 NIV

I Belong to God's House

Now you know God.
You're not a stranger to Him.
You belong to Him.

Have you ever felt like you just didn't quite belong? It must have seemed awkward—like you didn't fit in. That can be really tough. Everyone wants to have friends and to be part of a group.

God wants you to be part of the right crowd. That includes people who are saved and who desire to serve Him. People who are born again all belong to the house of God. That's the best group to belong to.

Maybe you've heard the saying "You plus God make a majority." So even when no one around you knows Jesus, you still belong to the right group. Jesus is with you, so you don't ever need to feel alone. Turn to Him for the friendship you need. Proverbs 18:24 is a reminder that Jesus sticks closer than a brother. Be sure you stick close to Him, too. Because you belong to Jesus, you're no stranger to Him. He loves you and will never let you down.

Whisper of Wisdom

Now therefore ye are no more strangers and foreigners,
but fellowcitizens with the saints, and of the household of God.

EPHESIANS 2:19 KJV

Brushing Up on Job Detail

Many hands make light work— guess how old that advice is!

What if your toothbrush had only one bristle? You could brush your teeth a lot better if lots of other bristles joined in to get the job done. God invites you, princess, to do just that, to be another "bristle" in the brush.

Just ask Moses how every bit of help makes a big difference. As Israel's leader, Moses tried to take care of several million people by himself. Then his father-in-law, Jethro, observed that Moses was going to wear himself out if he continued as the lone "bristle" in the toothbrush. Jethro suggested adding lots of other "bristles" by asking capable men to help him.

When it comes to tasks around your house, will you pitch in? If you toss the salad or fill the water glasses when the meal's about ready, your assistance will brush away someone else's stress. The cool thing is to offer your help when a lone "bristle" is wearing down. God invites you, princess, to brush up on ways to help around the house.

Whisper of Wisdom

"They will share the work with you. . . .
Then you will be able to keep your strength."

Exodus 18:22–23 NLV

Need a Rest?

Are you tired of always trying to be someone you're not just to impress everyone else? Come to Jesus, and He will give you the rest that you need!

If you're exhausted from trying to say and do the right thing all of the time so that your friends will like you, you need a rest! If you're one of those people who never shares your true feelings with anyone and bottles everything up inside because you're afraid your friends won't accept you as you are, you need a rest! If you're just plain tired of trying to live up to everyone's expectations, then you need a rest!

Jesus wants you to come to Him and be real. He wants you to be who He created you to be. You can be yourself in the presence of your Savior. He wants to know how you are feeling about everything, and He loves you and accepts you no matter what—just as you are! Lay all of your burdens down at the feet of Jesus and curl up for a long rest in His loving arms.

Whisper of Wisdom

Then Jesus said, "Come to me, all of you who are weary and carry heavy burdens, and I will give you rest."
MATTHEW 11:28 NLT

Runaway

Our heavenly Father is always watching us.

*B*e careful with that," Maria told her friend Jennifer as the girls played in Maria's room. "My dad gets really mad when we twirl batons in the house."

Jennifer whipped her baton around her back. "I'm the best majorette on the block. Nothing's going to hap—"

Her words were cut short by the sound of shattering glass as Maria's bedside lamp crashed to the floor. The girls stared at each other in shock.

"Oh no! My dad will be home any minute!" Maria cried. Sure enough, car tires crunched in the gravel driveway outside the window.

"Um. . .I just remembered my mom told me to come home and finish my homework early today. . . . Gotta go!" Jennifer rushed out the back door just as she heard Maria's father enter the kitchen.

Jennifer stood outside the door, her heart pounding. *No, this isn't right,* she thought. *I can run away from Maria's father, but I can't run away from God. He sees everything. He knows I did it. I can't just leave Maria to take my punishment, no matter how scared I am.*

Taking a deep breath, she turned around and reached for the doorknob.

Whisper of Wisdom

Where could I go to escape from. . .your sight?
PSALM 139:7 CEV

Nothing Can Separate Us!

He loves me. . . . He loves me not?

Come on, now, be honest. Have you ever messed up so badly that you wondered if your parents (or friends) could go on loving you? Have you ever just felt grumpy? Hard to get along with? Unlovable? Sure, we all go through those times.

Here's the thing about human beings—we mess up. A lot. We say we love people; then we don't behave like it. We act like we're best friends with someone one day, then move on to a new best friend the next.

God isn't like that. He doesn't change His mind. When He says He loves us, He means it. He loves us—forever and always! And there's nothing you can do to change that. Nothing. On your best day, He's right there, loving you. On your worst day, He's right there, loving you. Absolutely nothing can separate you from the love of God that is in Christ Jesus!

Whisper of Wisdom

For I am convinced that neither death nor life, neither angels nor demons, neither the present nor the future, nor any powers, neither height nor depth, nor anything else in all creation, will be able to separate us from the love of God that is in Christ Jesus our Lord.

ROMANS 8:38-39 NIV

Make a Wish

How many candles will be on your cake this year?
You're growing up fast! Take some time to enjoy your youth.

*T*here's something magical about growing up. Getting taller and looking older. . .becoming a young woman instead of a little girl. . .having others notice how mature you are. But while you're waiting anxiously for your next birthday, don't forget to enjoy the girl you are *right now*.

This is a wonderful time in your life! There's so much to discover about yourself. Your unique personality. . .your special talents. . .the outstanding qualities that make you who you are. Use this time to grow and develop into the young adult you will become. Spend time getting to know your heavenly Father and seeking His will for your future.

Growing up will happen on its own. And once your youth has passed, you can never reclaim it. So enjoy being young! Be silly and playful! Squeeze as much fun as you can out of your childhood. And when it's time to blow out the candles on your next birthday cake, wish for a year as great as this one.

Whisper of Wisdom

Let no man despise thy youth.
1 TIMOTHY 4:12 KJV

Growing Up

*Growing in our faith and our love for
one another is growing up in Christ.*

God loves it when your faith grows so that others notice it and want to know about it, to know how they can get what you have—the strength and peace that come from living in Christ. Then you can explain to them how you believe in God and what He has done for you and for them by sending His Son to be our Savior. God loves it when you grow from trying to care about others to truly loving other people and wanting them to know about God.

You don't start out as a grown person. You start as a baby; then you go through childhood to become a teenager and finally an adult. You learn a lot as you grow.

As a Christian, you begin as a baby, too. God wants you to grow as you learn more about Him. He wants you to become what He intends for you to be—His princess.

Whisper of Wisdom

*We ought always to thank God for you, brothers, and rightly
so, because your faith is growing more and more, and the
love every one of you has for each other is increasing.*

2 THESSALONIANS 1:3 NIV

Cookies with Character

*You aren't a cookie-cutter creation. The master craftsman,
God, put thought into every eye color, fingernail, and freckle.*

Every year Lanndrie looked forward to the one Saturday in December that was set aside for a huge cookie-making blitz with her grandma. They'd spend all morning mixing batches of cookies—everything from cutouts and sugar cookies to chocolate chip and peanut butter.

Lanndrie always took extra care to make sure her cookies came out uniform and neat—each cookie looking exactly like the one next to it. Grandma, on the other hand, liked a little bit of variety.

"I love how the top of this Christmas tree bows to one side," Grandma said as she looked at her cutouts on the cookie sheet. "It gives it character and makes it interesting."

God loves the details He put into our creation. Whether it's the cowlick in the middle of your hairline or the birthmark in the shape of a horse on the top of your foot, God crafted every part of you and every part of your personality. Praise Him today for your unique blessings!

Whisper of Wisdom

*You made all the delicate, inner parts of my
body and knit me together in my mother's womb.
Thank you for making me so wonderfully complex!
Your workmanship is marvelous—how well I know it.*

PSALM 139:13–14 NLT

Walk in Love

Love as Christ loves. Give as God gives.
Be a sweet-smelling savor.

Jessica was the new girl in the class, but she wanted to make new friends. She approached a group of girls who were laughing and sharing stories. A girl named Sophie appeared to be the leader. Jessica thought it might be fun to be in this circle of friends. However, as she approached, the girls became quiet. She immediately sensed that she was unwanted.

As she lowered her gaze and began to walk away, one of the girls stopped her. "Jessica, wait!" said Tara. "Would you like to sit with me at lunch?" Jessica hesitated, so Tara continued. "Don't worry about Sophie and the others. They're really great girls, and they'll open up. Sometimes they just forget how to share God's love."

At that moment Jessica could feel God's love through Tara's friendship. She smiled, ready to return the sweet-smelling savor.

Whisper of Wisdom

Walk in love, as Christ also hath loved us,
and hath given himself for us an offering and
a sacrifice to God for a sweetsmelling savour.

EPHESIANS 5:2 KJV

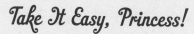

Take It Easy, Princess!

"Just a little dab will do ya!"
That's a quote from an old advertisement.
You might want to ask your grandpa what product this was.

Your mom or dad is too wise to do this, but what if one of them decided to drive the car into the garage going 65 miles per hour? Whoa! Way too much power, right? Did you know words are also powerful? It's a wise princess who knows how to avoid a disaster when she speaks.

When somebody asks a question, an edgy response gives the listener an unwelcome jolt. Whoa, way too much power! Why create a potentially hazardous situation by charging ahead with sarcasm, anger, or impatience? God invites His princess, instead, to put others at ease with a gentle answer. Your thoughtful reply can easily take the conversation as far as it needs to go.

So how much power will you use when your parent asks if you have homework tonight? Just remember, a little dab will do.

Whisper of Wisdom

A gentle answer turns away wrath,
but a harsh word stirs up anger.
PROVERBS 15:1 NIV

A Clanging Cymbal

Clack, clack. . .clang, clang. . .bam, boom.
What's all that racket?

Have you ever played around with band instruments? Have you heard the sound of a gong or a cymbal all by itself? Neither makes a very pretty sound all alone. It's kind of an annoying sound to many. The gong and the cymbal sound much better along with the rest of the instruments if played in the correct place during a song.

God's Word tells us that if we don't truly love people, we are only gongs and cymbals. Yikes! No one wants to be an annoying sound in other people's ears. So what should we do? We have to learn how to love others the way that God wants us to—unselfishly. We need to try to put others before ourselves. Yes. . .even your little brother! Is there someone in your life who is really hard to love? Maybe a girl at school or a relative or even your brother or sister? Ask God to change your heart toward that person. Ask Him to fill you up with love for other people.

Don't make a racket; learn how to love!

Whisper of Wisdom

If I speak in the tongues of men and of angels, but have not love, I am only a resounding gong or a clanging cymbal.

1 CORINTHIANS 13:1 NIV

Believing the Impossible

And the walls. . .came tumbling down!

*H*ave you ever faced a huge obstacle—one so big you couldn't see around it? You couldn't climb over it? Maybe you have a learning disability. No matter how hard you work, you still struggle to make good grades. Don't get discouraged. Choose to believe that God is bigger than that learning disability. Don't place any limitations on Him. . .or you!

There's a cool story in the Bible about some huge walls surrounding a town called Jericho. The people of God marched around those walls for seven days, and guess what happened—they fell down! (The walls, not the people.)

What if we prayed the walls down in our lives? If we looked beyond our limitations and saw ourselves the way God sees us? If we refused to give up when things went wrong? If we prayed in faith?

The next time you're going through a really hard time, remember that God is a God of the impossible. (That's right—the Bible says He delights in doing the impossible!) So even if you're facing a huge obstacle, choose to believe—and watch those walls come tumbling down!

Whisper of Wisdom

By faith the walls of Jericho fell, after the people had marched around them for seven days.

HEBREWS 11:30 NIV

Nothing but the Truth

Even if you tell part of the truth, it's still the truth. . . . Right?

*Y*our best friend wants you to tell a little white lie. Okay, not even a little white lie exactly—just not the whole truth. She wants you to stay overnight at her house, but before you end up there, she has other plans. And you know your parents wouldn't approve of those plans. "It's no big deal," she tells you. "Just leave that part out. It's not like you're lying. You'll still be spending the night at my house. What your parents don't know won't hurt them."

But you know deep down exactly what your half-truth would do. It would disappoint not only your parents, but God, too. And to disappoint your parents and God *would* hurt them. You'd not only let them down; you'd break the trust that you've worked so hard to build up.

When the temptation comes to leave out parts of the truth, remember that even half-truths can hurt others. Ask God for His wisdom when you have important decisions to make. He won't ever lead you in the wrong direction—guaranteed!

Whisper of Wisdom

Stop lying to each other. Tell the truth. . . .
We all belong to the same body.
EPHESIANS 4:25 NLV

Beautiful Creation

Think of it—God loves you so much that He created you in His own perfect image!

Have you ever wondered what God looks like? The Bible says that humans are created in His own image. Maybe that means He has characteristics like a body with arms to hold His children and legs to walk beside them. Maybe God has a face to show emotion, eyes to portray warmth, and a mouth to smile brightly.

God made us in His image because He wants us to identify closely with Him. Of all the beings He created in the beginning of time, He loved us the most and showed that love by placing a little bit of Himself in the way we look.

God looks at each of us and sees the beauty of His creation. No matter what you like or dislike about yourself, your heavenly Father sees the beauty of heaven in you.

Whisper of Wisdom

Man is made in God's image and reflects God's glory.
1 CORINTHIANS 11:7 NLT

Peace, Princess

Be a peacemaker, not a peace breaker.

$\mathcal{D}$o you find that you and your friends sometimes argue over really silly things that only lead to hurt feelings on both sides? Or do you ever fight with your siblings about some stupid thing and get so mad that you don't talk for days?

Arguments can break up friendships and disrupt families. And if that makes you feel bad, it must make God feel even worse.

Jesus tells us that peacemakers are blessed and they will be called children of God (Matthew 5:9). So, daughter of God, the next time it looks like an argument is about to begin with one of your friends, or a brother or sister, or anyone else, try being a peacemaker. Take a deep breath and—before you speak—think about whether this argument is worth losing a relationship over. It's not.

Princess, be a daughter of God. Do all you can to settle things peacefully. You'll feel better, and so will your King!

Whisper of Wisdom

Don't have anything to do with foolish and stupid arguments, because you know they produce quarrels.
2 TIMOTHY 2:23 NIV

Thanksgiving Day

Christians have much to be thankful for.
Every day should be filled with thanksgiving!

In 1620, the Pilgrims, who had been suffering for their religious beliefs and practices, set sail for the New World. After they arrived and began to start a new life, they realized they had much to celebrate. They had built homes in the wilderness, they had raised enough crops to keep them alive during the long winter ahead, and they were at peace with their Native American neighbors. They had beaten the odds, and it was time to celebrate and give thanks.

We celebrate Thanksgiving for many of the same reasons. We, as Christians, are thankful to God for our freedom to worship Him freely and openly. We are thankful for the rich blessings He has provided. We are thankful for safety and security. We are thankful for the family and friends who surround our table and fill our hearts. Consider, today, what you have to be thankful for, and then give thanks with your whole heart.

Whisper of Wisdom

Give thanks to the Lord, for he is good.
His love endures forever.

PSALM 136:1 NIV

Your Wish Is My Command

You don't have a genie.
But you do have a heavenly Father.

Once upon a time, a young man found a magic lamp. When he rubbed it, a genie appeared in a puff of smoke and offered the lad three wishes. He could have anything he wanted, simply by asking for it.

As a child of God, you have something far better than a genie. You have a heavenly Father who has the power to give you anything you ask for. As the Owner of the universe, He wouldn't find it at all difficult to reach into His vast treasure-house and grant your wishes. But unlike the genie in the lamp, God has *your* best interest in mind. That means He won't give you anything that would be bad for you, no matter how much you think you want it.

Don't be shy about asking God for the things you want. Go boldly to Him in prayer and make your request. Then rest assured that as long as what you're asking for is good for you, sooner or later it will come to pass.

Whisper of Wisdom

And all things, whatsoever ye shall ask in prayer,
believing, ye shall receive.
MATTHEW 21:22 KJV

Imitating God

Walk like Him. Talk like Him. Be like Him.

Girls like to imitate one another, don't they? They usually copy the really popular girls—the ones they want to be like. Have you noticed it—girls dressing alike so they can feel like part of the crowd—or talking alike so they "fit in"? If you're going to be a copycat, you need to do it God's way. He wants us to imitate Him! We are to be (and act) more like God, and there are many ways to do that!

How do you imitate God? Start by reading the Gospels (Matthew, Mark, Luke, and John) to see what Jesus did—then go around doing what He did. For example. . .He was kind to the people whom most others were not kind to. (Can you do that?) He didn't treat one person better than another. (No playing favorites!) He cared for the sick and the hurting and needy and poor. (Can you care for those in need?)

If you want to imitate Jesus, be a good deed doer! What a great copycat!

Whisper of Wisdom

Dear friend, do not imitate what is evil but what is good. Anyone who does what is good is from God. Anyone who does what is evil has not seen God.

3 JOHN 11 NIV

Princess Party Favors

You don't even have to wait for a party to hand out these special favors, but please note—you can't find them just anywhere.

Your family can have lots of fun holding a home movie night, but a little argument can easily get into the mix. Natural, sure, but maybe not as necessary as you think. That's why God asks you to hand out His special party favors.

With God's help, give the favor of a non-"me first" attitude by cheerfully letting someone else sit in your cozy chair. Patience is another super party favor to share generously when a bathroom break interrupts the moment of suspense. Be sure to stock up on the favor of bearing with the person whose head blocks your view, and that doesn't mean growling! A polite request will do fine.

The best thing about God's party favors is that when you hand them out to others, you will be pleasantly surprised when others in your family pass them out to you. God loves to see His princess handing out party favors. So stock up for your next movie night.

Whisper of Wisdom

Be completely humble and gentle; be patient,
bearing with one another in love.

EPHESIANS 4:2 NIV

A Gift from Dad

*Gold wrapping paper, ribbons, and bows. . .
I wonder what's inside!*

*I*magine Christmas is coming. You see all of the presents under the tree—especially the one wrapped in the pretty gold paper with your name on it. You try to guess what's inside. Maybe it's a new camera or some great new jeans. You can hardly wait!

Finally, Christmas arrives. One by one the presents are opened. You reach for the package and tear away the paper, only to discover. . .a stinky old tennis shoe!

What? You look at your parents, confused (and a little hurt). What kind of parents would give their daughter a gift like that?

Maybe this is a silly example, but here's the truth: Your parents give you good gifts—not dirty old sneakers—because they love you! They give you the things you need—and the things that bring a smile to your face. And here's the cool part: God gives even better gifts. . .if you ask! That's what the Bible says! Why? Because He loves you! So ask, princess! See what your Father has in store for you.

Whisper of Wisdom

*If you, then, though you are evil, know how to give
good gifts to your children, how much more will your
Father in heaven give good gifts to those who ask him!*

MATTHEW 7:11 NIV

Shining Armor

Yes, you are a princess. You're the daughter of the King.
But be the knight in shining armor, too.

As God's daughter, you might have thought you'd be pampered like the princesses in the fairy tales, and you know something? God *does* take care of you. He will meet your every need. He'll be with you each step that you take.

Just like in the stories, there is an enemy and a very fierce battle. Unlike a delicate princess, though, you aren't supposed to sit back in a fancy dress and watch. You have to be prepared when Satan—the enemy—attacks.

God has prepared some special armor for you. He gives you His Word as a belt to hold your battle clothing in place. Your heart is protected by the breastplate of righteousness (being "right" with God). Your feet are covered by shoes carrying the Gospel. Your faith is your shield to guard against doubt and temptation. The salvation of God covers your head, and the Bible is your sword. Faithfully wear your armor, and you'll be victorious in the fight. You can wear your beautiful robes once you reach heaven.

Whisper of Wisdom

Wherefore take unto you the whole armour
of God, that ye may be able to withstand in
the evil day, and having done all, to stand.

EPHESIANS 6:13 KJV

Pampered Princess

You're not spoiled. Just well taken care of!

God is famous for taking care of His children. He kept baby Moses safe in his basket on the Nile and protected Daniel when he faced the lions. He made David the shepherd boy a great king and blessed the childless Hannah with her very own baby, Samuel, and then five more! God has done wonderful miracles to help His children when they needed it. And He's just the same today!

As a daughter of the King of heaven, you are greatly loved. God watches over you night and day. He sends His angels to protect you. He warns you away from evil and disciplines you when you need it. He instructs you in the fine art of being a royal princess so that you can bloom and grow to become just like Him.

Wherever you go and whatever you do, remember who God is. The Creator of heaven and earth. . .the King of the universe. . .the Giver of life. . .and best of all, your very own Father.

Whisper of Wisdom

*My God shall supply all your need according
to his riches in glory by Christ Jesus.*
PHILIPPIANS 4:19 KJV

We're on the Same Team!

If family members stick together, the glue is strong.

Shannon thinks she's all that," Dena whispered to her gymnast friend Sara as they waited to perform their vaults. "But I can do more back handsprings than her any day of the week."

"Isn't Shannon your cousin?" Sara asked in surprise.

"Yeah. But since she got a gold medal on beam, she struts around like she's Shannon *Miller.*"

"She's doing what Coach told us to do—glide with confidence. Don't you want her to do well to help our team win?"

"I guess so," Dena admitted, her lower lip puckering into a pout.

"Then. . .what?"

"I don't know. I guess I get jealous sometimes. The highest I ever medaled was silver."

"I remember," Sara said, squeezing her friend's wrist. "And I remember how happy Shannon was for you."

"Yeah, she was," Dena agreed, glancing at Shannon practicing her floor routine. "Maybe I need to look at this a different way. If Shannon and I help each other, we both win, but if we pull in different directions, *everybody* loses. Maybe God wants us to learn to be on the same team in gymnastics so we can be better teammates in real life."

Whisper of Wisdom

It is truly wonderful when relatives live together in peace.
PSALM 133:1 CEV

Inside and Out

While others are looking at your outward appearance, God is looking at your heart. Which one deserves more of your effort?

It seems as if everywhere you look, you see the faces of beautiful people: on TV, in movies, on billboards, in magazines. . . But what do those people look like on the inside? Are they just as beautiful in their words, attitudes, and actions? Or is their outward appearance their best feature?

God says, "Man looks at the outward appearance, but the Lord looks at the heart" (1 Samuel 16:7 NIV). That doesn't mean you aren't to take care of your physical appearance, but that isn't to be your main focus. What makes God happy is when His children work on making themselves beautiful on the inside so that the things they say and do show His love.

Take some time today to read God's Word and talk with Him. Ask Him to make you beautiful inside so that others will see Him reflected in your life.

Whisper of Wisdom

"I the Lord look into the heart, and test the mind.
I give to each man what he should have because of his ways
and because of the fruit that comes from his works."
JEREMIAH 17:10 NLV

The Love Test

Ready for a pop quiz?
Don't worry—there's only one question!

Question: How do you show God that you love Him?

Answer: Obey!

Yep, that's it. Obey. Jesus told His disciples, "If you love me, keep my commandments." Ouch. So the next time you say, "I love you," to your mom, it might be a good idea to follow it up by obeying her. Or the next time a grandparent or parent says, "I love you, honey," and you respond with, "I love you, too!" remember those words carry a lot of meaning (and with those words come actions to prove it)!

So is love all about obedience? Isn't there more to it? Sure. To love someone means you're completely dedicated to them—that you will care for them. . .always. Love is a commitment. (Every princess should understand this word, because commitment to your heavenly Father is important when you live in the Royal Family.)

If you love, you obey. If you love. . .treat others better than yourself. If you love. . .make your bed. If you love. . .do your homework. If you love. . . Well, you get the idea. Obedience isn't always easy, but it is always right.

Whisper of Wisdom

"If you love me, you will obey what I command."

JOHN 14:15 NIV

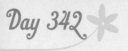

Two Commands

Jesus came to set you free from lists and lists of rules.
Now He asks for love above all.

𝓕lip through the first five books of the Bible, and you'll find list after list of rules and regulations for God's chosen people, the tribe of Israel. The Ten Commandments are just the beginning. Within the pages of Old Testament law, God's people received instructions on virtually every part of their lives, such as how to settle disputes, offer sacrifices, farm the land, and even prepare food to eat. Most of the laws started with the words *do* or *do not*.

Jesus came to free God's people from the choke hold all of these rules had on their lives. His two-part message was simple to understand: Love God. Love others.

Christ came to earth to offer freedom through His sacrifice on the cross, but the biggest enemies of His message were the most religious people of His day. They wanted to hang on to the Old Testament laws and follow them to the letter. Such attention to detail left no room for the love Jesus preached.

Thank God for His love today, and share that love with someone else. Then you'll be living out Christ's commandments to the fullest.

Whisper of Wisdom

Jesus said, "'Love the Lord your God with all your passion and prayer and intelligence.' This is the most important, the first on any list. But there is a second to set alongside it: 'Love others as well as you love yourself.' These two commands are pegs; everything in God's Law and the Prophets hangs from them."

MATTHEW 22:37–40 MSG

A Rule to Follow

Obeying your parents pleases the Lord.

Sometimes life doesn't seem fair. Like when your older brother gets to stay up until eleven o'clock and you have to be in bed by nine. Or when, because of the bathroom schedule, you have to wait until your older sister gets out of the shower before you can get in to brush your teeth. But those are the rules of the house, ones your parents set for a reason and you would do well to follow.

So when your parents tell you to do something—even when you think they're letting your siblings get the best of all deals—obey them, keeping in mind that that's what God wants you to do.

He put your parents in charge for a reason. They are older and wiser. And they have the enormous responsibility of teaching, watching over, and guiding you. They want you to be the best child you can be, a child God is happy with. They want you to be the princess God created you to be.

Even though things may not make sense now, they will when you have children of your own, ones you hope will obey the rules you make. For now your job is to obey Mom and Dad, remembering that they love you. And so does God.

Whisper of Wisdom

Children, obey your parents in all things,
for this is well pleasing to the Lord.
COLOSSIANS 3:20 NKJV

Infected. . .Eew!

Who wants to get an infection? Eew. . .gross!
Don't let someone else's bad attitude infect you!

*T*he Bible is clear on the kinds of people with whom we shouldn't be close friends. God's Word warns us not to be best friends with other girls (or boys) who have a really bad attitude. Why? Because a bad attitude is more contagious than the flu! Boys who are angry all the time, or disrespectful to their parents and teachers, or girls who love to gossip don't make very good friends, either.

This doesn't mean that you should be snobby and never talk to these people. They need to see the difference that Jesus is making in your life. Just be careful how much time you spend with kids like that, and pray for them to come to know Jesus. Nobody wants to get an infection. . .so make sure you and your friends aren't the ones spreading it!

Whisper of Wisdom

Don't hang out with angry people; don't keep company with hotheads. Bad temper is contagious—don't get infected.
PROVERBS 22:24-25 MSG

A Princess Asks, "How Much?"

When you're learning measurements in school,
will your teacher allow you to bring any stick for a ruler?

If your mom asks you to measure laundry soap, wouldn't it be silly to use a ruler? To see how much you've grown, would you get the thermometer? You'll get better results when you use an accurate measure. That's why God offers His princess the correct measure to use when you forgive those who hurt you.

To grab for popular opinion about how you should react will give you only inaccurate information. If you reach for the get-even tool, it'll be tempting to dish out what's been dished out to you. If you latch onto the rod of resentment, you'll end up hurting yourself even more. Only God holds the correct measure.

Over-the-top forgiveness is what God, through Jesus Christ, offers you. Nothing short of that, undeserved as it is. Will you offer the same to others?

Whisper of Wisdom

Forgive one another as quickly and
thoroughly as God in Christ forgave you.
EPHESIANS 4:32 MSG

Always on His Mind

God thinks about you all day, every day.
He cannot stop thinking about you.

You're on His mind every day all day—every night all night. He's thinking about you when you wake up in the morning, when you bite into your turkey sandwich at lunch, and when you fall exhausted into your bed after ball practice at night. God's thoughts about you cannot be numbered.

It's one of the many amazing facts about God. He can think about you every moment of every day, the same way He thinks about the other billions of people on the planet. Each thought is just as special as the next—He loves each of us that much.

Your heavenly Father eagerly waits for the time you spend with Him in prayer. He's been gearing up for your conversation since the last time you talked. The sad fact is that sometimes we're too busy with our lives and we don't give Him the time and attention He wants and deserves.

Spend time today preparing for your prayer time by thinking about the Creator. Praise Him for how He is working in your life, and thank Him for His blessings. He's thinking about you, too.

Whisper of Wisdom

How precious are your thoughts about me, O God.
They cannot be numbered! I can't even count them;
they outnumber the grains of sand! And when
I wake up, you are still with me!
Psalm 139:17-18 nlt

Erase It!

God's forgiveness is like a giant eraser. When you say, "I'm sorry, God," that's the end of it. He forgets about it, and so should you!

Okay, so you messed up. But there's still a positive side to your wrongdoing. *No way! Nothing good could come out of this!* you're probably thinking right about now.

I really did it—big-time! I feel low, and once Mom and Dad find out, I'll be grounded for eternity. There's no way I'm going to get out of this—it's trouble with a capital T. I don't think I'll even be able to forgive myself.

Even though you've done wrong, there's something wonderful to come out of all this, and that something wonderful is the forgiveness we receive from the Lord. After we say, "I'm sorry, God," we're immediately forgiven. He doesn't say, "Wait awhile; I'm really mad at you for this," or "I can't forgive you for this." He says, "You are forgiven, and I love you." He'll never bring it up again. If our mighty God can erase it from His mind, so can you!

Whisper of Wisdom

He has removed our sins as far from us as the east is from the west.

PSALM 103:12 NLT

Tasteful Words

Words are more powerful than they seem.
Choose them wisely.

*O*h, how many words you have from which you may choose. For the most part, if the words are used properly, there is nothing wrong with them. Your speech tells a whole lot about the young woman you are. It isn't just about the vocabulary you choose, either. In reality, that's a rather minor part. The tone of your words is perhaps more important. For example, if you are using God's name reverently and worshipfully, that is wonderful; but if you use it mockingly or flippantly, your speech becomes sinful.

The ability to communicate is a great gift from God. Be sure you use it to be kind and helpful. Don't waste this blessing on gossip, arguments, or unkind remarks. Let people see Jesus even in the way you talk.

Whisper of Wisdom

Let your speech be always with grace, seasoned with salt,
that ye may know how ye ought to answer every man.

COLOSSIANS 4:6 KJV

The Parent Party

*You are invited to the party of the century!
It's your mom and dad—having the time of their lives!*

Trying to figure out the perfect gift to give your mom or dad this Christmas? Something sure to make them happy? Try wisdom. It's an awesome gift!

No, you don't need to give them wisdom; you need to get it—for yourself. The wiser you are, the happier your parents will be. What does it mean to act wisely? Make great choices! Treat your brothers and sisters as you would want to be treated. Don't insist on getting your own way. Do the things you're told (without having to be told twice). Offer to help out when your parents are tired. These are all things that prove you're very, very wise.

But where does wisdom come from? Why, from your heavenly Father, of course! All you have to do is ask, and He will give you wisdom. Read His Word (the Bible). It's loaded with tidbits of wisdom. Then pray. Ask His opinion about absolutely everything. This is by far the wisest thing you can do.

The wiser you are, the more your parents get to party!

Whisper of Wisdom

*A wise son brings joy to his father,
but a foolish man despises his mother.*

PROVERBS 15:20 NIV

Growing Pains

Growing up in your walk with Jesus is not easy.
Sometimes it even hurts as you are stretched and molded.
But Jesus promises that the painful growth is a necessary
part of becoming the person He wants you to be.

When a girl is maturing, she often feels aches and pains in her legs or arms called growing pains. They are pains that she must endure in order to grow into a woman. The walk of a Christian is the same. When trying to grow and develop in the faith, a Christian must suffer different kinds of aches and pains that will grow her into a mature believer.

But God doesn't want you to go through this pain and gain nothing from it. When you allow the Lord to minister to you while you hurt, His touch is soothing like the loving touch of a mother to her daughter, and you will begin to feel better. These strokes of love are healing you and growing you to be more like Him. Come to God during those times when you need Him, and let Him soothe you with His grace, love, and peace.

Whisper of Wisdom

"Anyone who listens to my teaching and follows it is wise. . . .
Though the rain comes in torrents and the floodwaters rise
and the winds beat against that house, it won't collapse
because it is built on bedrock."
MATTHEW 7:24-25 NLT

The Great Adventure

Do you love a good adventure? If you're a Christ-follower, you're in for the adventure of your life!

Are you the kind of girl who loves mysteries and adventures? Always looking for something new and exciting to do after school? Then you'll love this: Following Jesus is the most exciting adventure *ever*!

The Bible tells us that God has a plan for each one of our lives (Jeremiah 29:11). He already knows what He wants us to do. It's a complete mystery to us, though, because He doesn't come right out and tell us where to go to school or which person we should marry or what we should be when we grow up. But He does tell us that when we pray, He will listen, and when we seek Him with all our hearts, we will find Him (Jeremiah 29:12–13).

All we have to do is put our trust in God each day, and He will show us His will, little by little and day by day. We never know what tomorrow will bring, but that's okay, because God does. When we "deny ourselves" and put Jesus completely first in our lives, an adventure awaits around every corner!

Whisper of Wisdom

Then [Jesus] said to them all: "Whoever wants to be my disciple must deny themselves and take up their cross daily and follow me."

LUKE 9:23 TNIV

The Way the Wind Blows

Jesus is as predictable as the wind. We know that when He moves, the effects will be evident in our lives.

You can't see wind, but you can certainly see its effects. The wind blows and proves its power by leaving behind broken tree limbs and other sorts of damage. The effects of Jesus can be compared with the blowing of the wind. We can't actually see Jesus move in the life of a believer, but we can see the effects of His presence there.

The wind is predictable; we know what will happen when it blows. The same is true of the presence of Jesus. We know that when we ask Him to move in our lives, He will. He promises to answer our prayers. We may not be able to predict His timing, but we can have faith that the outcome is already decided and that He will answer our prayers in His timing and according to His will.

Whisper of Wisdom

*"Keep on asking, and you will receive what
you ask for. Keep on seeking, and you will find.
Keep on knocking, and the door will be opened to you."*

MATTHEW 7:7 NLT

Minding Your Own Business

There are things you know. There are things you do.
Be sure it is your business.

You've been entrusted by one of your friends with a bit of private information. She shared the knowledge with you, believing you would keep it to yourself. That's one confidence you should never break. It might be juicy gossip that your other friends would like to hear, but it's not their business. If you're a good friend, you won't repeat things that aren't meant to be shared.

Is gossip something you have trouble with? Discuss your weakness with an adult you trust. Then turn it over to God. He will help you overcome this dangerous habit. It could be that you have too much time on your hands. If so, you should find an activity to fill those idle hours. Maybe if you took music or art lessons, tried a fun sport, or did volunteer work, you would have less time to gossip. Whatever you do, just make sure you keep your hands busy—not your mouth!

Whisper of Wisdom

Study to be quiet, and to do your own business,
and to work with your own hands.

1 Thessalonians 4:11 kjv

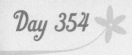

Insomnia

Even in the darkest of nights,
don't be afraid—God is awake.

What would you do with all your extra time if you didn't have to sleep? Would you spend more time on homework? Maybe you'd make a nightly trip to the mall to do some shopping. Maybe you'd spend more time with friends and family, or perhaps you'd end up vegging longer in front of the TV or playing more video games.

God's daily schedule doesn't include sleep. In the quiet solitude of night, God watches over His children as they rest. And in the brightness of daylight, He's watching just the same. Some people give credit to guardian angels for keeping us safe, but the writer of Psalm 121 knows better: "He will not let you stumble; the one who watches over you will not slumber" (v. 3 NLT).

In the dark and in the light, God is working in the lives of people on earth. His days and nights are the same, completing His will until He sends Jesus back to earth to bring His children home to heaven.

So rest easy, princess. God is watching over you—day and night.

Whisper of Wisdom

He will not let you stumble;
the one who watches over you will not slumber.

PSALM 121:3 NLT

The Princess Path

A detour may reveal a moment of beauty,
otherwise missed.

*T*he shortest distance between two points is a straight line. And although it seems right to find the quickest way to get to your destination, sometimes God may ask His princess to do the opposite. *You mean go out of my way?*

It's a sure way to demonstrate God's love to those living under the same roof. Putting care for others ahead of convenience seems senseless. Yet Jesus did that when He left heaven to come to a smelly Bethlehem stable. Jesus went still further out of His way to die for the sins of the world. By far, Jesus did not take the convenient route.

Will you go out of your way? When you're heading to bed tonight, cheerfully turn around when your mom calls you back to take a basket of laundry. Better yet, offer to come back for more! Going out of your way really does hold a moment of beauty for everyone.

Whisper of Wisdom

Let us not love with words or tongue
but with actions and in truth.

1 John 3:18 niv

Show Your Faith

Share the good news with everyone.

God wants you to share your faith in Him with others so that you will grow to fully understand every wonderful thing Christ has given you.

One way to share your faith is by living it every day! There are many ways to do that. You could get involved with service activities at your church—like helping with clothing handouts, making up food baskets for those who are hungry, or working at a shelter. You can also set a Christian example by being nice to everyone at school—not just your circle of friends.

Another way to share your faith is by bringing your friends to church and openly talking to them about how much Jesus means to you and what He has done for you.

As you do all of that, you will be pleasing Christ, sowing the seeds of His love, and winning others to Him one soul at a time! And best of all, you'll fully realize how good your own life is with Christ in it!

Whisper of Wisdom

I pray that you may be active in sharing your faith,
so that you will have a full understanding
of every good thing we have in Christ.

PHILEMON 6 NIV

Cyberspace Conduct

Computers open a whole new world of communication.
But with that privilege comes a big responsibility!

Do you like to IM your friends? Have you visited a chat room lately? Do you have your own *space* online?

While all of these options can provide a limitless amount of fun, at times correspondence can cross the line and become harmful. You most likely have observed a comment that could only bring pain and tears to the one it's written about. Sometimes people use the excuse that it was "all in fun" or even that it "isn't as bad as in person." Yet the pain is just as real.

Ask God for help in guarding your fingers as you type those words to your friends. As Proverbs 20:11 says, consider whether your motives are "on the up-and-up." Are you building someone up or tearing them down? Once the words leave your computer, they can inflict damage that you aren't able to repair.

Think of the other person as someone whom God created and loves. When you think that way, it's more difficult to key in those harmful words.

Whisper of Wisdom

Young people eventually reveal by their actions
if their motives are on the up and up.
PROVERBS 20:11 MSG

Does Your Gift Get Rave Reviews?

Is the true value of a gift all wrapped up in the present? Hey, what do you think?

You already felt uneasy about the gift you brought to the birthday party, but after seeing what the girl next to you brought, you're ready to run, wondering how you can hand *your* gift to the guest of honor. What's a princess to do?

Maybe that's what the woman in Bible times felt before plunking her measly gift into the temple treasury. *The people ahead of me must be giving enormous gifts.* Yet this woman mustered up the courage to stay in line and give God what she could. As Jesus observed all of this, He surprisingly honored the woman and her gift above all the others. Who would have thought?

Jesus must give rave reviews to the one who courageously gives what she can and refuses to be wrapped up in herself. So, princess, will you, like the woman who gave all she had, stay in line to offer your best to God regardless of what others might think?

Whisper of Wisdom

"But a poor widow came and put in two very small copper coins, worth only a fraction of a penny."

MARK 12:42 NIV

The Princess Stays Tuned

*By changing radio stations, you may forget
to switch back to your original choice.*

A radio station doesn't want to lose you during an upcoming commercial, so the announcer often says, "Stay tuned." It's the station's way of letting you know it will be back with more. How much more does the God of heaven want you to "stay tuned" while you wait for an answer to your prayer?

While you wait, God invites you, princess, to trust Him to get back to you in His timing. Expect Him to come through even though you don't know if it will be shorter than a commercial break or much longer than you'd think. And while you're waiting, keep expecting God to answer your requests.

Where else can a princess find such a cool place to lay down her request? Expect God to get back to you with the answers.

Whisper of Wisdom

*In the morning, O LORD, you hear my voice; in the morning
I lay my requests before you and wait in expectation.*

PSALM 5:3 NIV

Everlasting Gift

The packages we open on Christmas Day are nothing compared to the gift God gave us two thousand years ago—a tiny baby named Jesus.

When Kaitlyn was little, Christmas meant surprises, secrets, mystery, and presents, of course. Every year she scoured holiday toy ads, flagging every new toy and gadget she wanted. For little Kaitlyn, Christmas was all about *her*.

When Kaitlyn turned six, she started doing extra chores around the house to earn money to buy Christmas gifts for her family and friends. Sure, she still liked getting presents, too, but she soon figured out that she liked giving even more than getting. *Christmas,* she thought, *is about others.*

At age ten, Kaitlyn gave her life to Jesus at a week of church camp. Throughout the summer and autumn, she couldn't wait for Christmas to come again. She knew this year she would finally understand Christmas as God meant it to be—a celebration of Jesus' birth. Kaitlyn spent the weeks leading up to the holiday doing typical Christmassy things—decorating, baking, making gifts for others—but all the while focusing on the baby Jesus. *This year,* she thought, *it's not about me. And it's not about others, either. It's about the greatest gift I'll ever receive—Jesus. God, please help me to always be thankful for this precious gift. Amen.*

Whisper of Wisdom

For a child has been born—for us! the gift of a son—for us! He'll take over the running of the world. His names will be: Amazing Counselor, Strong God, Eternal Father, Prince of Wholeness.

ISAIAH 9:6 MSG

Devoted to Devotions

*Sometimes, too much of a
good thing can be too much.*

A young girl decided that she needed to begin to have daily devotions. She was so committed to them that she didn't miss one day in ten years. Not one day! And then, one day, she forgot. It was a perfectly normal day, and there was no real reason for the oversight. But she awoke the next morning and realized that she had failed.

After contemplating it all day, she began to feel a sense of relief. Legalism had taken over her zeal to be with Jesus, and it was more about the law she created for herself than the joy she got from the task. She learned that God didn't love her one bit more if she spent an hour reading the Bible every day. Or one bit less if she was just too busy to barely cry out for His help before her feet hit the floor in the morning.

What matters to Him is our love for Him, our desperation for Him. He wants us to want Him.

Whisper of Wisdom

*I have hidden your word in my
heart that I might not sin against you.*
PSALM 119:11 NIV

This Is a Test. . .

Good things come to those who wait.

Have you ever been through a really rough time—a time when you just kept waiting for something good to happen but wondered if it ever would? The Bible tells us that our troubles are a test of our faith. They teach us patience.

A daughter of the King has to learn to be very patient. But what does that mean, exactly? To be patient means you can wait calmly for something to happen. You don't get all worked up about it. Waiting isn't always easy—especially if you're going through a hard time—but it is possible!

If you want to find out about someone who learned to be patient, read the story of Job in the Old Testament. Talk about a guy who went through struggles! He had to wait a long time for good things to happen and went through lots of faith tests. (Most of them were like pop quizzes—he never saw them coming!)

Patience, princess! Learn from Job, and don't let those struggles get the best of you!

Whisper of Wisdom

My brothers and sisters, when you have many kinds of troubles, you should be full of joy, because you know that these troubles test your faith, and this will give you patience.

JAMES 1:2-3 NCV

Cherished

Feeling unloved? Crawl up onto your heavenly
Father's lap and be cherished!

Do you have any idea how much God loves you? John 3:16 tells us how much: He gave up His only Son and let Him die on a cross for you so that you could be with God forever in heaven. Do you still feel like you're not all that lovable sometimes? That maybe God couldn't love you because of all the bad things you've done? It's not true!

When Jesus died on the cross, He took away all of your sins! God has seen everything you've ever done wrong, and He knows about all of the bad things you might do in the future. . .but He loves you anyway. He wants to show His love to you every day. Do you feel His love? If not, think about crawling up onto your heavenly Father's lap.

What does it feel like to be held by God? He cherishes you! That means He tenderly cares for you. He knows everything about you and loves you anyway. He waits for you to come to Him each day!

Whisper of Wisdom

The Lord must wait for you to come to him
so he can show you his love and compassion.
ISAIAH 30:18 NLT

Strong Friendship

*God doesn't want you to go through life alone.
Hold tight to your friends, and they'll help you through tough times.*

If you're lucky, you have a handful of close friends who know everything about you—even the unlovable stuff—and still love you no matter what. God calls this kind of unconditional love *agape*, and it's the kind of love He wants His children to experience and give.

Friends are important during good times, but they become even more valuable during difficult times. As strong and independent as we think we are by ourselves, God knows an individual cannot stand up to the problems of life alone. That's when true friends offer encouragement, prayer, a hand to hold, and a shoulder to lean on.

Developing such a strong bond with a friend takes time and effort. But our close relationships with others and our unconditional love for them are one way we begin to understand God's love for us.

How are you showing your friends agape love? Spend time today thanking God for your friends and the love He offers through them.

Whisper of Wisdom

*By yourself you're unprotected. With a friend you
can face the worst. Can you round up a third?
A three-stranded rope isn't easily snapped.*

ECCLESIASTES 4:12 MSG

The Magic Wand

Do you ever wish you had a fairy godmother?
Surprise! You've got something better—a heavenly Father!

Remember poor Cinderella? She was invited to the ball but couldn't go because she had nothing but rags to wear. Then her fairy godmother appeared with a magic wand and transformed her into a beauty fit for a prince.

Do you ever feel like you need a transformation? Maybe you're doing things that you know you shouldn't. Maybe you know that God isn't proud of the way you've been acting lately. Don't despair! Just like Cinderella's fairy godmother, your heavenly Father can transform your sinful rags into a sparkling white robe of righteousness. And best of all, the "magic" doesn't end at midnight. God's transformation is powerful enough to last a lifetime.

If you have sin in your heart, why don't you ask God to forgive you? Then stand back while He uses His awesome power to turn you into a princess in His kingdom.

You'll live happily ever after!

Whisper of Wisdom

Anyone who belongs to Christ has become a new person.
The old life is gone; a new life has begun!

2 CORINTHIANS 5:17 NLT

Contributors

Janet Lee Barton has lived all over the southern United States, but she and her husband now live in Oklahoma. Janet loves being able to share her faith through her writing.

Cheryl Cecil lives in Fort Wayne, Indiana. Two married daughters and three granddaughters inspire her to write for girls of all ages. She loves finding any reason to celebrate life.

Debora Coty is an internationally published freelance writer, columnist, and author, who also teaches piano and serves as children's church coordinator. Look for her historical novels *The Distant Shore* and *Billowing Sails* for ages twelve and above.

Rebecca Germany is a resident of rural Ohio and has been an editor of Christian fiction for the past fifteen years. She enjoys having numerous nieces and nephews and working with church music.

Jennifer Hahn is a freelance writer, compiler, and proofreader who lives in Pennsylvania's Amish country. She and her husband, Mark, have two daughters and a son.

Gale Hyatt has been writing since the third grade. She and her husband live in Valrico, Florida, with their two handsome sons and one precious princess.

Kelly McIntosh is a full-time editor. She makes her home in Ohio with her husband and twin son and daughter.

Nicole O'Dell, wife and mother of six, is an accomplished writer of books, devotions, and Bible studies. She has been a Bible study leader and teacher for more than fifteen years.

MariLee Parrish lives in Ohio with her husband, Eric, and young children. She's a freelance musician and writer who desires to paint a picture of God with her life.

Rachel Quillin, her husband, Eric, and their eight children live on a dairy farm in Ohio. She enjoys gardening, writing, and spending time with her family.

Janice Thompson is the mother of four daughters and three granddaughters. She lives in the Houston area, where she spends her days writing, editing, and enjoying time with her family.

Annie Tipton is an editor and writer living in small-town Ohio. A former newspaper reporter, she loves her family, friends, sushi, and beach vacations.

Barton, Janet Lee
5, 12, 15, 22, 34, 50, 62, 85, 97, 112, 123, 139, 152, 160, 175, 188, 201, 214, 230, 241, 257, 265, 276, 287, 296, 310, 323, 331, 343, 356

Cecil, Cheryl
1, 9, 10, 18, 24, 27, 33, 37, 43, 49, 55, 59, 67, 75, 83, 87, 96, 102, 108, 114, 120, 128, 136, 148, 159, 165, 177, 189, 197, 209, 218, 223, 237, 239, 250, 258, 268, 282, 290, 298, 302, 305, 313, 318, 326, 335, 345, 355, 358, 359

Coty, Debora
30, 35, 40, 58, 69, 80, 100, 115, 129, 132, 154, 173, 193, 207, 228, 246, 266, 280, 320, 339

Germany, Rebecca
91, 137, 176, 191, 208, 222, 227, 261, 293, 314

Hahn, Jennifer
17, 45, 68, 82, 94, 109, 126, 135, 146, 153, 164, 178, 192, 200, 224, 249, 269, 301, 340, 357

Hyatt, Gale
2, 3, 20, 46, 66, 78, 92, 101, 122, 145, 161, 170, 182, 196, 213, 235, 244, 255, 274, 285, 311, 322, 333, 338, 365

McIntosh, Kelly
13, 28, 47, 76, 105, 130, 147, 163, 183, 247, 272, 278, 297, 329, 347

O'Dell, Nicole
29, 53, 60, 71, 74, 77, 86, 107, 124, 133, 144, 150, 158, 168, 184, 194, 199, 204, 219, 226, 232, 236, 251, 254, 260, 267, 288, 292, 304, 309, 316, 332, 350, 352, 361

Parrish, MariLee
7, 21, 42, 63, 84, 99, 116, 125, 141, 156, 174, 202, 216, 229, 242, 259, 270, 283, 299, 312, 319, 327, 344, 351, 363

Quillin, Rachel
8, 16, 25, 39, 51, 64, 72, 88, 95, 106, 110, 117, 134, 142, 155, 167, 179, 185, 190, 205, 212, 220, 233, 248, 252, 263, 277, 289, 295, 307, 317, 325, 337, 348, 353

Thompson, Janice
4, 14, 23, 31, 36, 44, 54, 57, 61, 70, 79, 90, 93, 98, 104, 111, 118, 121, 131, 140, 149, 157, 166, 172, 181, 186, 198, 206, 211, 215, 221, 231, 238, 245, 256, 264, 273, 275, 281, 286, 294, 303, 306, 321, 328, 334, 336, 341, 349, 362

Tipton, Annie
6, 11, 19, 26, 32, 38, 41, 48, 52, 56, 65, 73, 81, 89, 103, 113, 119, 127, 138, 143, 151, 162, 169, 171, 180, 187, 195, 203, 210, 217, 225, 234, 240, 243, 253, 262, 271, 279, 284, 291, 300, 308, 315, 324, 330, 342, 346, 354, 360, 364

Scripture Index

It's Time for Some. . .

Girl Talk

180 Q & A's for Life's Ups, Downs and In-Betweens

Popular blogging trio—mom, Nicole O'Dell, along with daughters, Emily and Natalie—offer trustworthy, biblically based advice for all your ups, downs, and in-betweens. Selected from actual questions they've encountered on their blog site, this fabulous resource offers real-life helps for issues including relationships, character, body image, fashion, gossip, and more. You'll find 180 questions along with answers and related scripture selections that will both encourage and challenge you in your faith walk.